One of the Toughest Parts of Parenting . . .

. . . is disciplining your children. *Don't Take It Out on Your Kids!* is a clear, concise guide that can help you understand what works and what doesn't—to avoid unnecessary conflicts and encourage your child's best behavior.

The sensitive parent knows that love and understanding are the keys to raising happy, well-behaved children. This book tells you exactly how to incorporate trust and mutual respect into your parent-child relationship—for truly successful parenting.

DON'T TAKE IT OUT ON YOUR KIDS!

A Parent's Guide to Positive Discipline

REVISED EDITION

KATHARINE C. KERSEY, Ed.D.

BERKLEY BOOKS, NEW YORK

DON'T TAKE IT OUT ON YOUR KIDS!

A Berkley Book / published by arrangement with
the author

PRINTING HISTORY
Acropolis Books edition published 1990
Berkley trade paperback revised edition / October 1994

ISBN: 0-425-14372-4

BERKLEY®
Berkley Books are published by The Berkley Publishing Group,
200 Madison Avenue, New York, New York 10016.
BERKLEY and the "B" design
are trademarks belonging to Berkley Publishing Corporation.

PRINTED IN THE UNITED STATES OF AMERICA

10 9 8 7 6 5 4 3 2

Acknowledgments

I am grateful to many people for their encouragement and support, but most especially to:

Cheryl Bunting, my doctoral student and friend, who spent many hours helping me think through the concepts in this book.

Susan Vorhis, my former student and longtime friend, who allowed me to come to Kentucky twice for extended visits in her home while we worked together to shape the contents of this book.

Kathy Northcott, my teaching assistant, who made sketches and helped me collect stories and anecdotes.

Sheryl Herbert Spence, who cheerfully helped with the typing when the going got rough.

Nancy Peterson, my student and friend, whose loving spirit inspired and helped me.

Tom Pinkston, a graduate student who gave flare and style to the book through his artwork.

All the students, parents, and children who have inspired me through the years with their questions and stories and who have provided me with the desire to help make the world a better place for children.

My husband, Wilbur, for his undying faith in me and his constant encouragement and support. Without him, I would have given up many times.

My children, Barbara Leigh, David, and Marc—who have taught me much and from whom I am still learning. They have truly convinced me that children are our "divine professors."

Contents

Introduction

It was Bob's night to put Paul, age 3, to bed. As usual, his son protested, thinking of a million reasons why he should stay up. Bob, who had been taking a parenting class, remembered the wisdom of giving the child a choice. He asked, "Would you rather walk upstairs, or be carried piggyback?"

Paul fell for it, answering eagerly, "Piggyback!"

Smug now that he had accomplished his goal, Bob got his son upstairs and went through the nightly ritual—the bath, the bedtime stories, and the good-night kiss. Finally he tucked Paul into bed and went downstairs to relax.

He had just settled into his comfortable chair and opened the newspaper when he heard a little voice coming from upstairs. "Daddy, Daddy, I've changed my mind! I've changed my mind, Daddy. I decided that I *need* to walk!"

Bob was taken off guard. His immediate reaction was the same as that of most parents. He tried to talk Paul out of wanting what he wanted—an impossibility!

"No, you don't, son. You don't need to walk. You made your choice. You can walk tomorrow night. It's getting late. Go to sleep."

Dad's response had given Paul encouragement. He might have a chance. At least he had Dad's attention. With this fuel, he climbed out of bed, went to the top stair, and started wailing loudly, "I *need* to walk. I have to go to the bathroom. I'm thirsty. I want to give you another kiss. You don't love me!"

He was pulling out the stopper and using everything that had ever worked in the past.

Bob tried feebly to counter these requests, but frankly was thrown by the intensity of Paul's behavior. Shortly, he gave in. "Oh, all right, come on downstairs and *walk.*"

The most amazing thing happened on Paul's journey to the bottom step! His personality did a complete flip. He changed in a split second from being an upset, crying child into a loving, docile, happy little boy. He ran to his father's chair, crawled up into his lap, stroked his face, and said sweetly, "You're *such* a good daddy. I love you *so* much!"

Bob thought to himself, "Isn't he wonderful? I do so love this little guy. Why can't he always be like this?" He reciprocated the tenderness and absentmindedly resumed reading the newspaper. A half hour later, Bob looked up and saw Paul playing quietly on the floor. *He realized that he had been had!*

Bob was mad. Angrily, he ordered Paul to "Get upstairs— and *fast!*"

Who was Bob mad at? Himself!

Who did Bob take it out on? His son!

Most parents have good instincts about what is best for their children. I believe they basically know what they should and should not allow. However, because they are tired and don't want to put up with an unhappy child, or because their child's anger makes them feel uncomfortable and/or guilty, they *don't follow through on their convictions.* Since they love their child deeply, they wage a constant inner battle between love and tender feelings versus frustration and powerlessness. They feel inept as parents. They are really disappointed in *themselves,* but they *take it out on their kids!*

That is what this book is about. It has been written for parents by a parent who took a lot of frustration, anger, unresolved hurts, and disappointments—without meaning to—out on her kids.

This book is written for parents who, like myself, have found themselves doing and saying things to their own children they don't like: things their own parents used to do and say, things they hated and vowed they would never do and say.

This book is written for any parents who want to become *conscious parents,* parents who have determined their goals for their children and are ready to identify some very important principles that will help them to accomplish those goals.

Our responsibility as parents is to help our children learn to live without us. Although the job really lasts a lifetime, the years of influence are very few. The average number of years when children and parents live under the same roof are probably about one-fourth of their lives. Realizing that these years will never come back, we parents need to spend them wisely, knowing that all too soon our children will leave us and go on to live lives of their own, based largely on what they have learned from us.

Since they come into this world totally helpless and would fail to thrive without us, our job as parents is to love and nurture them and to teach them how to live.

Discipline means "to teach and train." We need to be good

disciplinarians, to acquire skills that will accomplish the goal we set for ourselves, that of helping the child become a considerate and responsible human being.

There are several ways we can make children behave.

One is by using force. Another is by using fear. Still another is by using punishment.

Force will only work as long as the adult is bigger and stronger than the child. It does not lead to inner control, but rather makes the child angry, resentful, fearful, and dependent upon force.

Fear may work for very young children, since they are so suggestible and trusting. At some level, they realize that they are totally dependent on their caregivers, so they are afraid not to obey. In fact, they are so needy that they will work hard to get on the good side of the person whom they need the most, even if that person abuses them. A child will go to great lengths, sacrificing his own needs and wants to please and to make the world right for his parents. Fear can actually immobilize the child and can get him to behave in many self-defeating ways.

Punishment (inflicting pain for the purpose of hurting), can also be a strong motivator. The fear of punishment can keep a child from disobedience. However, there are many possible side effects that can result from punishment (see Chapter 3).

All three methods mentioned above (force, fear, and punishment) imply that the caregiver is superior and should overpower the child. Some adults feel that it is their job to "break the spirit" of a strong-willed child. They try to dominate and control the child until they see compliance and submission.

Even though these techniques might bring about quick results and instant obedience in the young child, they cease to be effective as she grows in age and in ego strength. As she matures, she tends to fear and avoid the adult who used such strategies. In time, she also loses respect for those on whom she was so dependent, which eventually leads to her separation and alienation.

There is another way to discipline children. Even though it may not appear to get the immediate results we might like, it is safer, more natural, and more humanistic. It is based on the assumption that children are by nature good, fair, and honest, and that they ultimately are capable of responding to that which is good, fair, and honest in us.

This method is based on mutual respect. It is treating the child as if he is as important a human being as you are. It is treating him with the same regard that you reserve for good friends and others whose love and friendship you desire. It is treating him with the same respect that you want him to give to others, to you, and to himself.

When you treat a child with respect, a wonderful thing happens. You develop a bond with her. An affectional tie binds the two of you in a warm and intimate relationship. This bond has a mysterious quality about it. It is inherently valuable to both persons, causing each to draw strength and energy from the emotional bond which exists between them.

Two important dynamics result: the child wants to please you and the child wants to be like you!

When there is a bond established between you and the child, discipline becomes easier and easier. As is true of a disciple, the child learns from the teacher, both by direct teaching and by modeling.

This book is an effort on my part to show how we can teach effectively without using force, fear, and punishment, but rather by treating the child with respect—the kind we have for ourselves and wish to hand on as a legacy to our children.

DON'T TAKE IT OUT ON YOUR KIDS!

Chapter One

Learning How to
Be Parents

Parenting is probably the most important job we will ever do, yet there is no preparation or training required. Anyone who is biologically equipped to reproduce can become a parent.

It is a known fact that many young girls get pregnant in order to have someone who will love and need them. They find themselves totally unprepared to deal with a crying, irritable baby who makes constant demands and gives little in return.

One of my students, who just completed her first year of motherhood, confided in me recently, "This has been an unbelievable year. Parenting is so hard. I think it must be the best-kept secret. If people knew what they are in for, there would be no next generation. I just stay confused and exhausted."

Since there is no prerequisite training required, most people parent in the only way that comes naturally to them—the way their parents did. Although much of what was done to us is long forgotten, it comes back to us—on an unconscious level—when we become parents. If our parents were yellers, hitters, moody, or withholding, then we become yellers, hitters, moody, or withholding.

By the same token, if we disagree with the way our parents behaved as parents, we might make a conscious effort to be different, or to take things to the opposite extreme. In either case, we are profoundly influenced by the previous actions of our own parents.

If we want to know how we were treated as children, we only need to examine our reactions to a child's crying, selfishness, or misbehavior. What do I feel like doing when a child throws his food on the floor? In my head, I know that this is normal behavior for a toddler. Do I respond as an adult to a child, by accepting his need to be a child and lovingly removing him or giving him something else to do? Or do I take it personally and resort to screaming, hitting, or flying into a rage?

If we find ourselves constantly irritable, not liking a child, or not being able to accept his "childishness," it has little to do with the child and everything to do with our past and the way our parents responded to our negative actions.

As children, we were born with our feelings intact. We were sensitive, alert, tolerant, forgiving, empathic, resilient, curious, and excited. At times we were also angry, afraid, jealous, and sad.

Very early, most of us learned that expressing negative feelings was unacceptable to our parents. To keep our parents happy or to stay in their good favor, we tried to cut these feelings off, to deny or repress them, until we were no longer in touch with that part of our personalities. By trying to repress our feelings, we eventually lost our ability to express them. Thus we became depressed, insecure, and anxious, feeling that something was missing in our lives.

It's as if we had closed a door on a whole part of ourselves (our negative emotions) and had thrown away the key. Thus we lost access to our true, integrated self.

Then we grow up and become parents. Suddenly the scene of our own early childhood is reenacted. Our unmet needs are still with us. Unconsciously, we lay this burden on our own children. We attempt to get them to fill up our emptiness—to be there for us—to give to us what our own parents could not or did not provide.

Because we were not allowed to express our entire range of genuine feelings, we do not allow our children to express theirs. When they are angry, sad, jealous, selfish, defiant, or afraid, we become anxious. It makes us feel out of control.

Then, in order to get control, we require our children to deny those feelings.

"Stop crying, or I'll give you something to cry about."

"Do what I say because I said so."

"That's silly. It was just an ice cream cone."

"There's nothing to be scared of."

"Of course you love your baby sister."

"Apologize to your father. Tell him you're sorry."

"We are at Disney World. You will have fun."

"Of course you'll share your toys and cookies."

"You will not talk back to me. Go to your room."

Because these strong feelings and emotions are so scary to little children (and unacceptable to us), children either act them out or sublimate them while they are young. As they get older, we see more obvious indications of the price children pay for this repression, such as self-defeating behaviors, defiance, and rebellion.

Suppose our children would comply with all our wishes. Suppose they stopped resisting us and became model children; good little boys and girls who never gave anyone any trouble. What price would they pay for their compliance?

When children give in to the attempts of adults to control their natural feelings, they lose themselves in the process. They lose touch with their needs, desires, intuition, and ability to think for themselves and make good decisions on their own behalf. Children who are too good are often numb inside, not knowing what they feel. They have shut down their own pain so as not to upset their parents.

These children look for someone else to run their lives, since their primary motive in life has been to satisfy the wishes of others. Most often, they become other peoples' doormats, for they do not feel that they deserve to be respected or loved in their own right.

Trying to control our children's negative feelings and actions takes many forms. Most of us fool ourselves into thinking that we are taking control for their own good. Therefore, we give ourselves permission to use whatever form of punishment it takes to get control.

We use coercion, force, insults, lectures, threats, criticism, fear, guilt, and spanking or hitting to bring about compliance. In general, we resort to the same methods our parents used. Unconsciously, we punish our children in exactly the same ways in which we were punished by our own parents.

If our children become violent and out of control, so do we. Ironically, many of us get out of control trying to teach our children to have control! Of course it never works, because children learn by example.

The truth is that whenever *we* lose control and disrespect our children by yelling, humiliating, and hitting, we are teaching them to avoid, fear, and hate us. All of us resist control by others, and children are no exception. When we attempt to exert our power over them, they have no choice but to become locked in a power struggle. They devote their energies to trying to get back, either actively by throwing things, hitting, and hurting, or passively by quiet disobedience or depression.

Passive-resistant people refuse to do things, find a way around doing them, do them slowly, badly, or not on time. They may comply in one area, but refuse in another. The most obvious ways that young children find to rebel against parental control are in the areas of toilet training, sleeping, and eating.

Passive children try to protect themselves from being controlled. As they get older, they rarely make decisions, but resist when others try to do it for them. They are notorious for having trouble with authority figures: bosses, teachers, police officers, or doctors.

Many of us do not like ourselves as parents. We are amazed and embarrassed at our own behavior. If we should happen to see ourselves on video or hear ourselves on tape, we are disbelieving!

One of the mothers in my parent class said this spring, "I can't wait until our children are out on their own—only two more years of all this hassle. Parenting is sure not what it's cracked up to be. All we do is argue."

"My children have turned me into a monster," another parent said to me recently. "I sound just like my father, and I hated him when he acted that way. I vowed I would be different."

If we find ourselves bottled up with anger, becoming enraged over minor happenings, or easily explosive, we need to go back and get to the root of our pain. Otherwise, we will not only frighten and confuse our children, but we will be teaching them unhealthy ways to express their feelings. If left unchecked, we can actually destroy their self-esteem and be a model for violence and abuse.

We need to get help for ourselves so we can stop this cycle from being passed on to the next generation. Help is available. The way out of the pain is through it. We have to recognize that we were at times unloved and treated unfairly before we can stop trying to earn love from ourselves as well as others. We must get in touch with our own child within and learn to identify, understand, and make peace with this complex history that makes us who we are today.

It is possible that our behavior has little or nothing to do with what our children are doing. It could be that some other area of our life is not working for us, and we are taking out our frustrations on the ones who are the most available and defenseless—our children.

Kent Hayes, in his book, *When Good Parents Have Bad Kids,* shares a personal story about his two-year-old. One day Dr. Hayes had picked up his son from the baby-sitter and hurried home to meet his wife so they could take the car to be fixed. She was an hour late in arriving home because of an emergency at work. By that time, he was furious because they had missed their appointment at the dealership. He huffed around, and they said unkind things to each other. She went upstairs and stayed a long time. Dr. Hayes took the child for a ride in the car to cool off. As they were riding, the two-year-old announced that he wanted to go back to the baby-sitter. "Why?" asked his father. "Because my house is broke," answered his son.

Children can sense when all is not well. Parents with serious trouble in their marriage who say they are staying together for the sake of the children are fooling themselves. Children cannot thrive on hatred and bitterness. They are not doing their children any favors by forcing them to share their living nightmare. Children cannot emerge from a steady diet of selfish, never-ending backbiting or silent wars with any degree of health and sanity.

That is not to say that parents should never disagree or argue. In fact, children need to see honest expressions of emotions in their families. They need to know that conflict exists when two or more people live together. They need to learn to resolve conflicts and solve problems.

But when arguments turn into personal attacks, they are no longer productive or healthy. When the intent of the participants is to hurt and to destroy, the child's foundation of trust will be shattered.

An old Chinese proverb states, "If we do not change our direction, we are likely to end up where we are headed."

It is difficult to learn to be an effective parent. It takes awareness, desire, and hard, honest work. It is humbling, to say the least, when we realize that our children become our teachers. They inspire us to grow and develop into more healthy, tolerant, and loving people.

I like what Jordan and Margaret Paul wrote in the preface to their book, *If You Really Loved Me:*

> To Our Children—
>
> By being who you are, you give us the opportunity to learn how to become more loving people. When we don't see your light, it's our vision that needs clearing.

If your house is broke, fix it!

Chapter Two

Bonding: The First Step

Babies come into the world already knowing how to communicate. They do not hesitate to let us know when they are upset, hungry, uncomfortable, sleepy, angry, sad, lonely, or bored.

Not only do they cry to let us know they need help, they also have the ability to smile, winning us over when we might otherwise feel like giving up on them.

Infants are not equipped to survive independently, but they are equipped to interact with others in ways that maximize survival. In other words, they are born with the mechanism to bond with those who love them and are responsible for their care.

Our job and responsibility as parents is to reciprocate with warm responsiveness, encouraging our baby's initial attempts at communication, and to attempt to meet her needs. In this way, we develop a bond, or an affectional tie of trust and acceptance, that becomes a model for all the other human interactions in her life.

We can bond with any child at any age, but the older the child, the more time it takes to build the necessary sense of trust. As long as our motive is to increase the child's feeling of self-worth, the quality of her life will be greatly enhanced by our efforts.

Once this bond is established between parent and child, the two are held together in a warm and intimate relationship that has a mysterious quality about it. The bond is inherently valuable to both, causing each to identify emotionally with the other.

When this bond between you and your child is cared for, nurtured, and treated with respect, an important thing happens: the child wants to please you and wants to be like you. This bond thus becomes the foundation for all future interactions between you and your child, including discipline. In this way, your methods of discipline—teaching and training—will be met with cooperation from a child who is already open, trusting, and eager to learn from you by your teaching and your example.

Children know they are valued when they have adults who value them. We show children that we value them when we give them ourselves—our physical and emotional presence (smiles, embraces, touching), and when we believe in their inherent goodness.

We all know how it feels to walk into a room of strangers. We feel awkward and ill at ease, until we catch the eye of a friend across the room. As his eyes light up, we feel relieved and our hearts become lighter—just to be recognized and validated.

That is what our children deserve to have from us every day. Whenever they "walk into our room," in the morning, or the afternoon, or night, they need for us to stop what we are doing and "light up." Smile, touch, show delight in the very existence of your child. Let him know that he is the source of your pleasure.

These special moments are what memories are made of, the memories that live in our heads forever and that no one can take away from us.

Every child needs at least one adult who is crazy about him and never gives up on him, who believes in him. Every child needs at least one adult who can't resist the urge to kiss his dirty face, hug, hold, and snuggle him for no reason, comfort him when he is sad or afraid, respond immediately when there is a problem.

We all want someone to love us as we are. The most basic need of a child is to be loved for what he is, not for what he can or can't do. When a child has this kind of unconditional love from one adult, this bond fills the emptiness in his heart and gives him the seed for a self-concept that will grow as he grows. This basic feeling of self-worth provides him with the enthusiasm, courage, and confidence he will need to carry him through life.

A child needs to feel that he is loved unconditionally. If he is only loved for what he can do, he will come to believe that he is a human "doing," not a human "being." He will feel that he must continue to *do*—to produce, to accomplish, to succeed, to excel—in order to receive love and acceptance. At first he will feel that he must work hard so others will approve of him, but eventually he will internalize this motivation, and only be happy with himself when he is "doing."

Such strivings most likely will lead him eventually to the path of perfectionism and/or depression. He will constantly be setting himself up for disappointment, gloom, self-hatred, or exhaustion, never be satisfied with the amount or level of accomplishment. Perfectionism leads to rigidity, prudishness, and/or psychosomatic illnesses.

Always feeling a sense of loneliness, this person frequently turns to an outside source (alcohol, work, drugs, cigarettes, food) for temporary relief in an effort to dull his senses or cover up the pain he feels inside. This addiction provides instant distraction from having to think and feel. Instead of choosing to become addicted to an outside source, some people choose to become addicted to the addict. These are the *enablers* or *codependents* in our society. These people basically have the same need—to focus outside themselves in an effort to numb themselves from the pain, emptiness, and basic dissatisfaction within.

The epidemic in our society today, I believe, is child *neglect*. We see symptoms of this neglect in crime, delinquency, suicide, and mental illness. It is not that children aren't having their physical needs met—although that is true in more cases than we want to recognize—but rather that children's *emotional* needs are being neglected. A child has no one with whom to bond, for he can't bond with a moving target.

Most adults are too busy, stressed, worried, and preoccupied to sacrifice the time and energy it takes to be there for the child. Children know us better than we know them. They watch, listen, and often successfully predict our reactions. They can imitate us to a tee. That is because they are so dependent on us, realizing that they could not survive without us. They need for us to be okay and will go to great lengths to protect and please us.

If we are sick, they are thoughtful; if we are grouchy, they feel responsible; if we are upset, they are helpful. They rise to the occasion for us. They are face-watchers. When they come into the room with us, the first thing they do is check our faces. They cue into our body language more quickly than our verbal language. They believe the way we act, not what we say.

We need to become better experts on our children. We need to follow their example and listen, watch, and learn to interpret their behavior. We need to accept their feelings, help them to learn to identify them, and teach them ways to cope with the wide range of emotions they experience from day to day and hour to hour.

We need to provide consistent, loving guidelines for them. We need to be fair, firm, and fun all at the same time. I stole those three words from Barbara Woodhouse, who trains dogs! I watched her demonstrate techniques on a television special and realized that animal trainers had developed a loving, firm approach that works for dogs. Why can't we see that children need the same kind of consistency so they can internalize the expectations we have for them?

Children deserve our undivided attention, one-on-one, every day. The wise parent will set aside time each day, fifteen minutes minimum, to spend listening to his child. This should be a time when there is nothing else that has to be done, when your child is free to call the shots and decide how you'll spend the time together: maybe a talk in the living room, sitting together in the "snuggly chair," or taking a walk outside. This time will come to be very special—to you and your child—when she can count on having your undivided attention.

If you have several children, stagger their bedtimes, and

offer them an incentive for leaving you alone while you spend time with their sibling. Children learn to respect this special time for another child when they know that their time is coming each day, every day. On the weekends, perhaps the time can be extended to an hour or two.

I know many families who are doing an excellent job of this. In one family, the father is the primary caregiver for three days and the mother for three. One day is a family day. In another family, the father gets the children up and takes them to breakfast every Saturday so the mother can have a free morning. These are the ways that bonds are cemented. When children know they are special enough for us to stop what we are doing, set aside time for them, even eliminate some of our "jobs," and block out other distractions, they feel important, peaceful about who they are, secure, loved, and validated as human beings.

Gradually, they internalize those feelings of self-worth, realizing that they deserve to be treated well by others. They can also afford to spend time and energy recognizing and meeting their own needs.

Each child is born with special gifts. When a child has bonded with or been validated by one adult, he is then free to discover those natural talents. His energy is unleashed, and he has the enthusiasm and courage he needs to follow his dreams and reach for the stars!

Chapter Three

Honoring Our Children

If we truly honor children, we will do everything within our power to *keep their spirits open.*

Our *spirit* is the innermost, intangible part of ourselves. It's who we are. It's the part of ourselves that makes us different from everyone else. It's the part of a person that touches another person without words or physical contact. It is the part of us that feels, and the part of us that determines our actions. *It is the driving force in our lives.*

When our spirits are *open,* we are energetic and happy. We are relatively free of anger. We are cooperative and want to communicate. We care about what other people have to say to us, and we have no need to hurt others.

When our spirits are *closed,* we feel uncomfortable and others can sense that something is wrong.

The Signs That Others' Spirits Are Closed to Us

They Are Lethargic and Resistant

One of the complaints I hear most about children from their teachers and parents is that they are "lazy." Children certainly are not born lazy. They have a great deal of energy to learn new things and to push their limits. When a baby wakes up, he is usually not interested in lying still in his crib until someone happens to come along. He cries, wiggles, moves around and protests, signaling that he is finished sleeping and wants attention.

I believe that the reason children appear to be lazy, is that their spirits have been closed, they have shut themselves down for preservation.

They Are Critical, Sarcastic, and Argumentative

When a child's world is not working for him, he often doesn't know how to express his sadness and anger. (He can't possibly know how if he hasn't had role models who freely and authentically talk about their own hurts and disappointments.) Some of the coping techniques most used by parents and teachers to mask angry feelings are the use of sarcasm, criticism, and arguments and children imitate these maladaptive behaviors.

They Avoid Eye Contact

When we feel good about ourselves and others, we usually have no trouble looking people in the eye. However, when our relationship is strained and the usual closeness is absent, we feel uncomfortable and ill at ease. Eye contact is hard to maintain. We have a need to look elsewhere so that the other person cannot see the hurt in our eyes, for fear that our broken spirit might be disclosed.

Their Facial Expressions Reflect Anger

Even a little child can detect anger in his mother's face. He will take her face in his hands and turn it toward him, if he is in doubt. He becomes frantic when anger appears on the face of one he loves and needs.

They are Sullen and Unresponsive

Babies who are not nurtured and validated can become so sullen and unresponsive that they actually fail to thrive.

Downcast looks, glassy stares and immobile faces are all familiar signs of depression and evidence that life is not working well for the individual who exhibits this kind of demeanor.

Their Tone of Voice Is Harsh and Sharp

When we hear the voice of a loved one on the phone or in the other room, we know instantly, by its tone, whether that person is okay or not. A baby will start crying when she hears anger in her mother's voice.

They Are Uncooperative

When children are disagreeable and disgruntled, they don't want to participate in activities with others. They find some fault with everything suggested to them, especially when they think someone else is trying to be helpful.

They Are Passive-Resistant

These people want others to read their minds. They are so afraid of being rejected that they find it hard to take risks or to let their wants and needs be known. They let others walk on them. They are compliant, and because their energy is blocked, they hold grudges and often plan revenge.

They Do the Opposite of What We Want Them to Do

When a child feels powerless—that she has little or no control over her life—one of the ways to get back at those who boss her around is to do the opposite of what is asked of her. If we want her to eat, she isn't hungry. If we want her to stop at four cookies, she is determined to eat eight.

We all can recognize the irritating traits listed above. We can think of friends, children, bosses, and colleagues who exhibit them in abundance. Perhaps we can even identify them in ourselves from time to time.

What is it that makes us *need* to develop such coping techniques? What is it that we do to children that makes it necessary for them to close their spirits to us?

Unfortunately, some of the parenting techniques that were used on us and that we hear of frequently from unaware or unconscious parents are the very ones that close our children's spirits.

Common Parenting Techniques That Close Children's Spirits

Criticizing

"You look ridiculous in that outfit!" "Your hair's a mess." Parents don't realize how tender their children's feelings are and how important it is for them to feel validated and accepted. It is hard to have good judgment and to make good decisions when others criticize the choices we have made.

Speaking Harshly

The tone of voice we use with children is more convincing than the actual words we use. When our voice denotes displeasure, disgust, or irritation, the child will find a way to back off so as not to incur further wrath.

Not Taking Someone Seriously

"That's silly." "Don't be so sensitive." "You know you like school!" Responses such as these indicate to the child that we do not validate his feelings, that they are unimportant and don't matter. A child will respond to this hurt by shutting down, and not venturing to explain himself in the future.

Being Sarcastic

Sarcasm and teasing hurt as much, if not more, than anger directly stated. Because they are often socially acceptable ways of dealing with animosity, many people think they can get away with these jabs that mask the real feelings lying beneath the surface. If the sender gets detected, he can always counter with, "I was just kidding. Can't you take a joke?" But the damage is done.

Embarrassing

Whenever I ask my students to write about a time when they were embarrassed as children, I am impressed with the accurate recall, the emotions and the details that come to mind. Sometimes, as they share these memorable experiences, tears begin to flow over something that might have happened forty years ago, which, to anyone else involved, may have seemed entirely harmless and insignificant. Often the effects have been devastating.

Being Rude

When a child is treated with disrespect, she responds by treating others in the same careless way. Furthermore, she assumes that she is unworthy—not to be admired—and so she fails to develop the traits of social responsibility, self-confidence, and mastery. Sadly, she fails to see, much less develop, her natural potential.

Taking One for Granted

It is so easy to take the people we love for granted. We expect them to be there, to love us, and to respond to our needs upon demand. It is especially easy to take children for granted. Because they *can't* leave us, we assume they will always be there for us. Sometimes our vision is so blurred that we fail to see them for the special and unique beings they actually are.

Forcing Our Will on Another

"Do it because I said so!" "Come here this minute." "Eat every bite!" Commands such as these alienate us from those who make such requests. None of us wants to be told what to do. The natural reaction would be, "No!" When we fail to recognize the desires and feelings of a child, we will most likely be faced with rebellion in one form or another.

How, then, can we become conscious parents? How can we help our children become responsible human beings without closing their spirits, yet still have some control? Is it ever too late to repair the damage we may have done?

I believe that inside all of us there is a drive to be healthy. That is to say, I believe that none of us is happy or content when we are not doing our best. When we are fully functioning, we are enthusiastic, energetic, and resilient. The way we can achieve such optimum health is by keeping our spirits open and developing the techniques that will help keep open the spirits of those we love.

The Traits We Need to Develop

It is not easy to develop traits that we did not observe in those who were our teachers. Most of us parent the way we were parented—or make a conscious effort to do the opposite if we didn't like the way we were raised. Therefore, for some, the following techniques will seem instinctive. For others, they will seem difficult and unnatural, and to acquire them will take more effort and determination. Trust me, it is worth it.

The Art of Being Gentle

Our children need to be cherished. They need us to handle their feelings with care, as we would a fragile package. When we realize how unique and special each child is, when we stand in awe of the precious miracle that our child represents, we will be more careful with our words and actions. We know without a shadow of doubt that if something happened to our child, our sadness would last a lifetime. When there is a crisis, we stop everything until we know that our child is safe. We need to give preferential treatment to our most precious possessions, not only when they are sick or in crisis, but every day.

The Art of Listening

Communication is the most important skill in life. Next to physical survival, the greatest need of a human being is psychological survival—to be understood, to be affirmed, to be validated, to be taken seriously, to be appreciated.

According to Alice Miller, author of *Prisoners of Childhood,* our children need to have at least one "enlightened witness" who values, believes, understands, and listens—really listens—with her ears, her eyes, and her heart. When a child's experiences have been validated, the child can deal with the difficulties of life.

Some suggestions for setting the stage for listening are:

- Go to a quiet, comfortable place where no one else will hear you and where there will be no distractions.
- Place yourself on eye level with the child.
- Be quiet and patient.
- Use the child's name. Touch him. Speak softly.
- Forget *your* perspective. Try to place yourself in the child's skin.
- Don't talk. *Listen!*
- Wait until your child is ready to talk. If necessary, help him with, "It's tough, isn't it?" "It's scary sometimes." "Life is hard." "I want to know what you are feeling."
- Watch the child's face and body language. When words and body language don't agree, believe the body language! A quivering chin or downcast eyes speak volumes.
- Give nonverbal encouragement and support. This includes eye contact, a smile, a hug, a wink, a pat, or reaching for your child's hand.
- Check your own tone of voice and body language. Make

sure that you do not come across as sarcastic, condescending, judging, all-knowing, or in a hurry.

- Make sure that your face and attitude convey warmth, gentleness, acceptance, and patience.
- Mostly *listen,* and when you speak, do so softly. Resist the temptation to talk, judge, explain, justify, preach, question, or moralize.
- Use encouragement to keep the child talking. This provides psychological air. If possible, let your child unravel his own problem and find his own solution. If necessary, after he has depleted his resources, *carefully* offer some perspective and problem-solving skills.
- Use a tone of voice and language that will reassure your child that you love him unconditionally and will be faithful to him always. Nothing he can say will sever the emotional bond between you. Show pleasure in his company. Be impressed by his accomplishments. Offer support for the difficulties he experiences.

The Art of Mirroring, Validating, and Empathizing

One of the most effective forms of communication between persons who care about each other is *focused dialogue.* It consists of three processes called *mirroring, validation,* and *empathy.*

Mirroring is the process of accurately reflecting the content of a message. The most common form of mirroring is paraphrasing. A *paraphrase* is a statement in your own words of what the message sent means to you. It indicates that you are willing to transcend your own thoughts and feelings for the moment and attempt to understand your child's perspective. For example, when your child says to you, "I don't want to go to school," a mirrored response would simply be, "You don't want to go to school. I see."

Validation is a communication to the sending person that the information being received and mirrored makes sense. Validation is a temporary suspension or transcendence of your point of view that allows the other person's experience to have its own reality. Typical validating phrases are: "I can see that . . ."; "It seems like . . ." "What you're telling me is . . ." "What I hear you saying is . . ." For example, "What you're telling me is that you wish you didn't have to go to school."

Empathy is the process of reflecting or imagining the feelings the sending person is experiencing about the event or the situation being reported. This deep level of communication attempts to recognize, reach into, and on some level experience the emotions of the sending person. Typical phrases for empathic communication include, "I can imagine that you must feel . . ." "When you experience that, I hear . . . understand you feel . . ." and "That makes sense." For example, "I can understand why you wouldn't want to go to school. It makes sense to me that you would feel that way."

The processes of *mirroring, validation,* and *empathy* affirm the other person and increase trust and closeness.

The Art of Touching

When we reach out and touch, we show that we care. Often words fail to express our feelings. A touch on the arm or back, or offering to hold a hand can convey a deeper message of warmth and caring, which every child needs.

The Art of Apologizing

All of us make mistakes. To err is human. However, it takes strength and integrity to admit our mistakes and apologize to those who are affected by our actions. Children are quick to forgive. They feel relieved to know that others can make mistakes. Furthermore, they learn that mistakes are a part of life. When we truly forgive, we start over—without a grudge—but a little wiser, because we make an effort to learn from our mistakes.

The Art of Not Giving Up

Every child needs at least one person who believes in him and does not give up on him. When a child has such a person, he will believe in himself. As long as we live, we have the power to change. Therefore, it is never too late. We need to convey to our children that we will never give up on them.

Chapter Four

Discipline Techniques That Don't Work

According to Webster, the word *discipline* means "to teach and to train by instruction." The word *punishment* means "to handle roughly, to injure, to hurt." Yet to many people the words mean the same thing: when they say that a child needs some discipline, they usually mean he needs a spanking. On the other hand, many also are convinced that not spanking means being permissive—having *no* discipline.

There are all degrees of spanking, from a swat on the behind to a severe beating with a belt or board. For most people who were spanked as children, a swat seems harmless and natural. They often use it as a means to "get the child's attention." They would argue that not to swat is letting the child get the upper hand, losing control.

I would suggest that neither spanking nor permissiveness is effective or necessary. In fact, both are humiliating, disrespectful, and insulting to the child. When parents are permissive, children grow up to be irresponsible, manipulative, and unpleasant. They think and act like the world owes them a living. Surely no parent wants to raise a child who is spoiled, demanding, and disrespectful. Parents who have such children indeed feel humiliated themselves.

In an effort then to show the child (and remind themselves) who's boss, many parents will resort to hitting (mostly because it was done to them and they don't have any other techniques in their repertoire; besides, they "turned out all right!"). Spanking does get results—if you are looking at immediate gains. It usually *does* stop the misbehavior for the time being. However, we must think in terms of the long-term effects of our parenting techniques. What are our goals for our children, and is this short-term action going to get us the results we want?

I would suggest that the opposite is true—that spanking a child has so many unpleasant side effects and can lead to so many serious problems, that even a swat on the behind is not worth the risk.

Since the home is the training ground for the future, and since our children learn their three most important roles in life (gender, spousal, and parenting) by watching the actions of those who parent them, it is our obligation to examine the possible implications of our behavior.

I would like to suggest the following as possible side effects of spanking—not meaning to imply that one or two spankings will ruin your relationship with your child or lead to every problem mentioned—but proposing that the risks are great enough for us to take them seriously.

At a time in history when we are being made aware daily of the problem of violence in our society, it only makes sense that we take an honest look at ourselves and ask, "Where is all that violence coming from? Where are our children learning it? Am I unwittingly doing anything to perpetuate it?" Surely we can't blame it all on television. We must realize that each time we hit or hurt a child, we are teaching him to do the same. Is the American home sanctioning violence by being its training school?

Children need to have role models who exhibit self-control, who handle their anger in constructive ways, and who settle their problems with their heads and not their hands. Most parents admit to feeling out of control when they lash out verbally or physically at their children.

Spanking usually results in resentment, revenge, rebellion, and retreat on the part of the child. It certainly does not cause the child to want to be near *or* to please the one who hit him. At best, it chips away at the bond of mutual trust and respect that is so necessary for healthy living and growing. Most children will resort to sneakiness ("I'll be more careful next time so I won't get caught") or turn the hurt inward and conclude, "I'm a bad person," thus reducing their self-esteem.*

When the child perceives that he is continually being treated harshly and unfairly, his hostility and anger become a part of his personality. He develops a tough exterior to avoid additional hurt and spends his energy trying to retaliate and seek revenge. If carried to the extreme (as it often is, even in

*Nelson, Jane, *Positive Discipline* (New York: Ballantine Books, 1981), pp. 13–14.

the "best" of homes), a child can become chronically depressed and neurotic.

The use of force also teaches children that "might makes right" and that it is acceptable for the strong to overpower the weak. Older children interpret this as a license to hit their younger siblings and pets. Isn't it interesting that hitting anyone other than a child is called "assault and battery" and is punishable by law?

As the child gets older, a swat or slap is likely to be interpreted as a joke. Therefore, in order to be effective, it must be more severe and painful. It can, and often does, of course, lead to child abuse. Usually the spanking does not stop when the lesson is "learned" (How would you ever determine this?), but when the spanker is tired or has spent his anger. This suggests that the benefit is greater for the one who is venting anger than for the one on whom the anger is being vented. Selfishly, by refraining from violence with our children, we could avoid the possibility that, in our old age, when we become dependent on our children, the roles might be reversed and our children could abuse or neglect us.

The right to hit those whom we love is an accepted family practice in 75 percent of American homes. Many people seem to think it is as American as apple pie and motherhood.

Domestic violence occurs in 50 percent of families each year, and 60 percent of parents admit to using physical punishment with their children. At least one-third of married couples feel that hitting a spouse is permissible.*

Some people feel that only wimps don't use force. (It is interesting to note that when the white man was moving West, the Great Plains warriors thought them barbarians because

*Hutchings, Nancy, *The Violent Family* (New York: Human Sciences Press, Inc., 1988), p. 17.

they saw them hitting their children, an unheard-of practice in Indian culture.)

Most people have not taken an objective look at the issue to enable them to decide for themselves whether or not it is a practice they thoroughly endorse and want to pass along to the next generation.

When parents resolve to stop spanking, they are forced to look for other alternatives for discipline, and, as a result, they usually like themselves better. When they learn other successful techniques for discipline, there is more communication and a better relationship between parents and children.

Studies have also shown that children who are not hit by their parents are more likely to find nonphysical ways to settle their differences with siblings and friends.

Violence is self-perpetuating. Once it is accepted in a family as a normal way of life, it is difficult to stop. The modeling theory seems to account for the continued use of spanking as a means of changing children's behavior. Parents who were hit frequently are the ones who generally use the most violence; those who were not hit, rarely resort to spanking. Violence creates victims who grow up to victimize others. Virtually all parents who are guilty of child abuse were once abused children themselves.

In Sweden, a law was passed making it illegal for parents to hit their children. Of course, the law is unenforceable, but the writers of the bill wanted to make the point that children just do not improve their behavior when they are hit or threatened. Their reaction is the opposite: they think in terms of revenge.

One can't help but be alarmed when looking at today's society and seeing the increase of violence in America, both in the home and on the street. New forms of violence—

"bashing" and "wilding"—have come to the attention of social workers and the medical profession. Although acts of terrorism and murder in other countries shock most of us, nowhere is there more violence between family members than in "peace-loving" America. In the eyes of many, it has become a national tragedy.

I have long been curious about behavior. Ever since my children were born, I tried to figure out what made them tick. I wanted to discover what made them do the things they did, and how I could change my own behavior in order to change theirs.

Whenever I took my children to the park, I watched what other mothers did when their children misbehaved. One day a little boy picked up leaves and threw them on top of my son's head. My son shrieked and the child's mother turned and saw what her son had done. Exasperated, she walked over to him and smacked him on the seat of his pants. Then she shrugged her shoulders and walked off as if she had taken care of the matter. I watched to see what her little boy did when she was no longer looking. This time, when her back was turned, he picked up the leaves and dumped them on my son's head again. Later I saw him go behind a tree and smack his little sister in the seat of the pants.

I learned a valuable lesson that day: children model our behavior. Even though the mother's intentions were good and she thought she was stopping her child from behaving inappropriately, she was actually teaching him to hit, as well as teaching him to be more careful when he misbehaved to make sure she wasn't looking.

Since those days when my children were very young, I have watched many methods being used by teachers, parents, baby-sitters, and other adults who found themselves in charge of children. I'd like to elaborate on some of the methods that I have seen people use that I believe backfire. In other words, they don't really teach the child to behave.

Embarrassing and Humiliating

There are many ways we can punish people. One is by inflicting physical pain, but another is by inflicting emotional pain. Embarrassing and humiliating a child is a cheap shot. It may get immediate results in that it stops someone's behavior for the time being, but it has no lasting results because of the unwanted side effects.

Someone who has been embarrassed or humiliated usually reacts by withdrawing (either physically or emotionally) or by retaliating. At the very least, the embarrassment leads to a dislike of and loss of respect for the one who embarrassed him.

Some people respond to embarrassment or humiliation by turning it inward. They dislike themselves, cry, become moody or sullen, or develop self-doubt or hatred.

At best, a person who is humiliated will reject the punisher and all that he stands for and values. So when we humiliate and embarrass, we run the risk of losing the respect and admiration of the person whom we embarrass.

If our goal is to help children learn to control themselves and to behave appropriately, embarrassing and humiliating will not help.

Ordering

When we order our children to do something, we create a conflict, a dislike, an urge to rebel, to test, or to challenge.

When we say, "Come here this minute!" the very nature of our order invites the child to challenge, "I can't come," "I'm busy," "I'll be there in a little while," anything to let us know that she resents our power over her. (Children are well aware of their status. They know that they are dependent and we hold the power. There is no need to rub it in, or alienate them by constant reminders.) When we order children around, we frequently get into power struggles with them. No one really wins in a power struggle. Each person is striving to save face and neither wants to back down.

Taking Away Favored Things

Another technique that many parents use to try to control children's behavior is to take away their favorite things. We threaten to take away their hobbies, make them stop Little League, dancing, sports, or take away their bicycle or television. We take away the car or make them stay in the house for a day or a week or two weeks. I have never known this method of control to be effective. Rather it sets up feelings of resentment and anxiety. Many times it is impossible to live up to the threats we have imposed on our children, and they know it. This makes us look ineffectual and causes the child to lose respect for us. We need to remember that children have the same feelings we have. Therefore, we have only to put ourselves in the child's place to see how it feels.

I like to read. That is my hobby. What if my husband suddenly decided that I needed to clean the house more thoroughly and told me that I could not read for pleasure until I had the house cleaned to his satisfaction? Do you think I would drop my reading and clean the house? Not likely. I would not develop any enthusiasm for cleaning the house because of his threat. Conversely, I would resent his method of manipulation and would go to great lengths to rebel, either actively or passively. I believe that children have the same reactions as we do, only they are more hesitant to protest openly and therefore may choose the route of misbehavior.

Labeling

Children live up to their labels. When we tell children they are lazy, they get lazier. When we tell them they are slow, they get slower. When we tell them they are fat, they get fatter. Children believe what they hear about themselves. They have tremendous faith in adults and in the perceptions that adults have. There are many ways we can use this to our advantage, however, particularly by helping the child hear good things about himself.

I used to tell my son he was a good duster. I told him no one could dust as well as he could, and I used to brag constantly about how shiny the furniture was when he dusted. Finally he said, "Aw mom, you're just trying to get me to dust." But it worked. When he wants to, he can get everything all shined up. I'm confident that he has a great deal of faith in his own ability to make a house sparkle.

Arguing

When we argue with our children, they realize that they have us hooked. They are getting our full attention, and arguments usually go nowhere. Oftentimes, when we go around and around in an argument, we lose our perspective, our cool, our rationality. We say many things that are foolish and inappropriate, immature, silly, sometimes damaging, and hurtful. Getting into arguments with our children is nonproductive. If we refuse to argue, there will be no argument. That's not saying that we can't discuss matters. Discussion is healthy, but arguing is counterproductive.

Fussing and Nagging

When we fuss and nag at our children, we usually make them mad. When someone fusses and nags at us, we get tired and arrogant. We are not motivated to improve our behavior, but rather we are motivated to stay stuck. If someone is constantly telling me that I burn the toast, I get so nervous about it that I'll usually keep on burning it.

I remember hearing someone at a retreat say, "My wife has been nagging me to give up smoking for thirty years. Since I've been here, no one has mentioned my smoking. I have had a chance to reevaluate it and I've decided I really want to quit. Therefore, I'm going to throw all of my cigarettes away! But, I bet when I go home, my wife will be angry that I gave up smoking while I was away from home."

Later, when we saw the man, he told us that his wife *had* been angry and said to him, "How come all those times I asked you to give it up and told you how damaging it was, you never stopped? Then when you go away, you decide you'll stop? How come?" He said, "I told her, 'It was because I got so tired of your nagging. Let's face it. I didn't *want* to please you. I didn't *want* to reward you!'"

Threatening

Many parents threaten all day long, "You won't get to go outside. You won't have your snack. You're not going to get to watch TV." But then they don't follow through. Sometimes parents threaten the impossible. "I'll never take you shopping again. You'll never go to the movies again. I'll never buy you any more clothes. I'll never wash your clothes again." We lose our credibility with our children when we threaten to do things that we never intend to do. We should be careful and count to ten or maybe twenty before we issue an ultimatum.

Repeating Commands

Many of us find ourselves saying over and over what we want our children to do, and they in turn tune us out, knowing that they will have many other chances to hear what we have to say. We want to get in the habit of telling our children only once what our expectations are and then following through. I've seen a parent repeatedly call a child to come inside. The child doesn't pay attention until his parent uses a tone of voice that means business. As soon as the parent has reached that level, the child immediately obeys.

Once I went to pick up my son who was swimming in a friend's pool. When I got to the house, I called to him to come. He didn't respond, so I went closer and called again. He still didn't respond, so I walked all the way to the pool and called him from the side of the pool. He came then and we left shortly after. When we got into the car, I said to him, "Why didn't you come when I called?" He said, "Because I didn't hear you the first two times." Obviously he *had* heard me, or he wouldn't have known that I had called a total of three times. He had told on himself and laughed. So did I.

Children are on to us. They know our level of discomfort, and when we mean it. We need to mean it the first time we say it. In other words, we need to think our words through *before* we say them and be sure we have the energy to back them up.

Pleading and Begging

Some parents act as if they're getting permission from their children to be parents. "Please, listen. Please obey me. Please do what you're told."

When we plead and beg with our children, putting ourselves at their mercy, they realize they have the upper hand and lose respect for us. It is important that we not convey the message to children that we are weak and unsure of ourselves. Our children need for us to be in control, to say what we mean, and back it up with action.

Scaring

Many parents use fear to get children to behave. Older siblings frequently try to scare their younger brothers and sisters to coerce them into doing what they want them to do.

Although sometimes these scare tactics work in that children will immediately obey, the long-range effects can be disastrous. A child might be so traumatized that his worldview may be forever affected.

Many children are being threatened with "I'm going to sell

you to the circus," "I'm going to send you to military school," or "I'm going to leave you at the mall."

Children have enough fears naturally without being told that bogey men, snakes, monsters, the devil, and ghosts are going to suddenly appear from nowhere to get them, eat them up, or snatch them away.

In time, children lose respect for those who manipulated them with fear tactics when they were vulnerable. Parents eventually lose their credibility with children when they try to control with these unfair and demeaning practices.

Inconsistency

Children often misbehave because they are treated inconsistently. When we remember that children repeat the behaviors that work and eliminate the ones that don't, we realize how important it is for us to react to their inappropriate behaviors the same way all the time.

For example, a mother came to me because she had trouble with her little boy getting into her bed each night. She confessed that she didn't mind, but her husband didn't want him there. When the child came into their room, if the father did not wake up, the child crawled in bed and slept between his parents. If his father *did* wake up, one of two things happened. Either the father took the child back to his own bed or the father slept elsewhere. We can see why the child continued to come into the room at night. The odds were in his favor. Two nights out of three he got to stay. One night he got plenty of room. These parents have actually *taught* their child to continue to come into their room each night to try to sleep with them. The parents' inconsistency has given this child the impetus to wake himself each night to see what would happen.

It is hard for children when their parents disagree. Children can adapt to different sets of expectations from different people, but they find it difficult when one parent changes his or her expectations from day to day: one day allowing a behavior to continue, perhaps ignoring it, and another day punishing the same behavior.

Giving a Child Everything He Wants

My definition of *spoiling* is giving a child something that is not in his best interest, or giving in to a child's demands, against our better judgment, just to keep peace.

The overindulged child is being taught that his wishes and needs come first. When we give in to his temper tantrums (crying, sulking, acting out), we fail to teach him a much-needed sense of responsibility. We deny him the joy that comes from learning to delay gratification and work for a goal.

We teach him to be selfish and self-centered, to think the world is his playground, and that he deserves to have whatever he wants.

We are setting him up for a lifetime of frustration and disappointment.

Power Struggles

We should never get into power struggles with our children since they are no-win situations. We need to be careful to make our rules fair and sensible, and we need to enforce our rules and let our children know that these rules are not negotiable.

That is not to say that we don't allow our children to think through issues, to discuss them with us, or to suggest alternatives—but the *way* to teach children to do this is very important. On one hand, we invite them to be reflective, questioning, responsible, thoughtful, and inquisitive. But on the other hand, we don't want them to be argumentative, disrespectful, challenging, nasty, and rude. These are hard concepts for a child to learn. We must be patient and consistent. We need to let our children know when we mean business, when we are open for suggestions, and when and how it is permissible for them to raise objections. The important issue here is that we do not encourage or reinforce our children when they behave inappropriately. If we refuse the bait when our child behaves in an inappropriate manner, she will quickly learn that this behavior is not acceptable, and it will not be tolerated or allowed.

Losing Your Cool

Children need someone older and wiser to be in charge. When adults resort to screaming, saying things they don't mean, falling apart, or losing their cool, children react in many different ways. When they feel that an adult is no longer in control, they are frightened. Children imitate our behaviors and when we yell and go berserk, they usually do the same. The tension escalates and nothing productive is accomplished.

Being Vague

Our children need for us to be clear, concise, and to the point. When we are vague, when we say, "Be good," "Straighten up," or "Be quiet," children really don't know what we mean. When we tell our child to clean his room, it may take him five minutes or five hours. His notion of cleaning the room might be quite different from our expectation. We need to let him know exactly what the job entails. We need to spell out specifically the behaviors we expect.

Sometimes we are vague because we are not sure ourselves what we really want from the child. It is best for us to wait until we are sure of what we want him to do, so we can be clear, concise, and to the point. We come across as being weak when we don't have the energy or fortitude to back up what we are saying, and our child will take advantage of that weakness and look for loopholes.

Allowing Dangerous, Destructive Behavior to Continue

It is very important that we *not* ignore major infractions of rules. After we have carefully set the rules we think are sensible and fair, we need to pay attention and stop the child immediately when these rules are broken. Allowing unacceptable misbehavior to continue or ignoring it only makes the child's behavior get worse.

Laughing at Misbehavior

Sometimes adults confuse children by giving mixed signals when they misbehave.

I have seen parents laugh at their two-year-old when she attempts to bite them, first treating it as a game and maybe even pretending to bite back. Then all of a sudden, the child leaves teeth marks on her daddy's shoulder, and the parent suddenly becomes irate. He may yell, smack, or (heaven forbid) bite the child on the shoulder to "show her how it feels." The two-year-old is totally confused. What was at first a game now brings wrath and pain.

A three-year-old has learned some naughty words from neighborhood children. He tries them out at the dinner table and the parents' immediate reaction is amusement. They look at each other and snicker. They may ask him to repeat what he said, and they laugh again. They tell him not to say those words anymore. Why shouldn't he? It caused his parents to laugh.

Some parents think it's funny the first time their teenage child drinks too much and comes home tipsy. They exchange knowing glances, as if their son is "growing up." He can certainly sense the mixed message their response conveys.

Rewarding Misbehavior

Inadvertently, most adults give attention to and thus reinforce many of the behaviors they would like to extinguish.

In the grocery store, when a child is tired and cranky, she starts crying for a candy bar. A parent is tempted to buy it just to get her to settle down and focus on something else long enough to complete the grocery shopping.

At home, when the twins start fighting at bedtime, their dad might promise to let them stay up another half hour to watch a special TV show *if* they stop fighting.

In these instances, giving our children something they want has immediate positive results in that it stops the undesirable behavior. However, the serious implication is that it teaches our child, *when I misbehave, my parents will reward me to stop.* Children then learn to behave inappropriately when they want something (a candy bar, to stay up later). This is the opposite message from the one we need to teach, which is, *I will get no reward for misbehaving.*

Breaking the habit of rewarding misbehavior is one of the hardest for adults to learn. It takes awareness, motivation, and hard work.

Allowing the Child to Manipulate the Adult

Unless parents are aware of the principles of behavior (children repeat the behaviors that work and eliminate the ones that don't), there is a tendency to allow children to manipulate the adult. Once children get the upper hand, they can become little dictators and develop obnoxious personalities.

When you are in charge, it is imperative that you make quick decisions about what you feel is best for children. That is what makes parenting so difficult—and exhausting.

Suppose you decide that your child should not sit or stand on tables. When she climbs up and tries to get on the table, you say, "No, you are not to sit or stand on the table." Then she continues to try—to cry, to beg, to complain. Finally she wears you down. You change your mind, "Oh well, what the heck! Who will it hurt?" You give up, turn your back, and act as if you don't notice that she has climbed on the table. She has learned an important lesson. She knows how to manipulate you, to get you to weaken: "If I cry, whine, complain, or persevere, I can get what I want."

Trying to Talk a Child Out of Wanting What He Wants

Remember the story about Bob and his son at bedtime. When parents are too tired, insecure, or indecisive to make a firm decision, they hope they can remove the conflict by getting the child to change his mind. (Bob tried to convince Paul that he didn't need to walk up the stairs.)

Good parenting is good decision-making. It requires us to be able to say no and make it stick.

Paul learned another unintentional but important lesson: when he is given two choices, he can have both. One he got right away, the other he had to work for.

Expecting the Child to Read Your Mind

Although children are perceptive and quickly pick up on the emotional state of those around them, they cannot read our minds. They need to be told, very clearly, what is expected of them, especially in new situations.

Many times parents wait until a child misbehaves to instruct him. When the family goes to Grandmother's for a visit, and Sarah announces that she doesn't like meat loaf and green beans, her mother becomes angry. When Grandmother offers to fix rice and Sarah agrees that she would like that, Mother scolds and threatens, "You cannot have any dessert unless you eat what is on your plate."

In this instance, the child has not been told ahead of time what is expected of her. It takes time and energy to think ahead and anticipate problems, but unless our children have been instructed how to behave, we cannot fault them for doing what comes naturally.

Putting the Child on a Guilt Trip

Some parents who find it hard to state their own wants and needs try to control children by making them feel guilty.

If Bob protests when he is asked to dry the dishes, his mother snatches the towel from him and dries them herself. She maintains a huffy attitude and refuses to answer him later when he asks if he can have a cookie.

When Jerry brings his report card home, he leaves it on the coffee table because he has two Ds and is afraid of what his father will do to him. When Jerome comes home, he looks at the grades and puts the card back on the coffee table. At dinner he refuses to talk to his son. He will talk to everyone else, but when Jerry asks him a question, he pretends that he doesn't hear. He looks the other way and changes the subject.

Many parents learn to control with guilt and continue to do so after their children are grown. If Marie and her husband, Ed, choose not to go "home" for Christmas, the next time Marie calls her parents, she hears an icy greeting at the other end of the line. She knows they are upset that she did not comply with their wishes at Christmas, although that subject is never mentioned again.

Children eventually move away emotionally and/or physically from those who put them on guilt trips—who "act out" their hurts and disappointments instead of speaking up. An even more serious side effect, however, is that they also will lack the skill of identifying and verbalizing what is wrong for themselves. Unless they learn to overcome this handicap, they will do the same to their children.

Chapter Five

Discipline Measures That Work

Since our goal for children is to help them become self-starters, highly motivated, and controlled from within, what are the techniques that parents can use to actually facilitate these goals?

Prevention is important, setting the stage for compliance and cooperation. A lot depends on parents being objective about their children's behavior and using self-control to keep calm and put things in perspective.

In describing discipline measures that work to move children from being externally controlled to being internally controlled, I have broken this chapter into three parts: What parents can do to control themselves, what parents can do to control their child's environment, and what parents can do to help their child learn self-control.

What Parents Can Do to Control Themselves

Ignore Minor (Annoying) Misbehavior

Each child is unique, with a personality of his own. This makes him special and different from others. He wants and needs to be accepted because of his uniqueness, not in spite of it.

This is why two children from the same family, born to the same parents, are often opposites. They have found ways to behave that make them distinct. If one child is dependable, a leader, responsible, and a good student, the other child might try to find ways to be the opposite, especially if the parents compare and reinforce competition between the two.

The answer to this dilemma, for the parent, is to avoid comparisons and to find ways for each child to be unique. This can be done from the time the child is very young. Parents can communicate to their children in many ways that they are loved because they are different. ("I love your brown hair." "You are special because you have freckles." "You are such a good duster." "You have a good math brain." "You can sing so well." "You have such a good sense of rhythm.")

Children should be allowed some slack. Because each child longs to be loved and accepted as an individual, they will often look for ways to show their individuality. For instance, while doing his homework, one may like to sit with his feet tucked up under him when he reads. Another may swing his foot as he studies. Still another may make little clicking noises as he does his work.

Or a child may develop little habits while he eats that could become quite aggravating, if the parent allows them to bother him. A child might prefer to eat with a spoon instead of a fork, or eat all of one food before he touches another. Another child might prefer to sleep with a night light on while his brother likes to clench up his fists or roll his eyes into the back of his head when he is upset or angry.

The wise adult will accept these differences without making them into annoyances. Usually, when we overlook these behaviors (act as if we don't notice), they go away. If they are not dangerous, destructive, or an impediment to learning, we can decide not to let them get in our way.

Think Before You Speak

One of the most important techniques parents need to implement is that of thinking before they speak. We are often careless and say what we think without realizing the implications: "You make me sick," "You'll be the death of me," or "I'll never take you to another movie (restaurant, shopping mall, concert)."

Our children take us seriously when they are young. Eventually they realize we don't mean what we say and by then, they lose faith in us. When we lose our credibility with them, they fail to respect us or take anything we say seriously.

It is sad to see parents who realize they have lost their effectiveness with their children. They feel powerless, helpless, and resentful. The children have the upper hand and have taken over the power. The adults are at their mercy. Think before you speak.

Tell a Child What Is Expected of Him and Only Say It Once

After we have thought through what we want to say to our child, it is important that we carefully make our expectations clear.

It helps to make sure we have his full attention. We may need to call his name, perhaps touch his arm as we talk with him, and speak softly.

Then tell him our message in language he will understand. Make sure it is clear to him. "Johnny, it is time for you to start picking up your toys." "Mary, it is time for you to turn off the radio and begin your homework."

Be Firm

We need to give our children our full attention if we expect them to take us seriously. We can't speak haphazardly or halfheartedly and expect obedience.

Sometimes when parents are unsure of themselves, not certain whether something is really a good idea or important enough to make a big deal over, children will sense their ambivalence and take advantage of the situation.

I've seen adults tell a child something very serious, but with a smile on their face. "Jasper, don't talk to me that way" (smile). "Sallie, don't you dare stick your tongue out at me" (giggle, giggle). In essence, they are verbalizing one message, but conveying the opposite nonverbally. It is estimated that 80 percent of our communication is nonverbal. For that reason, our children will take our nonverbal language more seriously than the words we say.

We need to get our own act together before we can expect a child to take us seriously. It is important that our words, attitudes, and actions convey the same message.

Follow Through

After we tell our child what is expected, it is imperative that we pay attention immediately to see that he obeys us. If we told him to wash his hands, we have to make sure that he does as he is told.

If you tell your child that he may not have a cookie before supper, you need to be sure that you mean it and will enforce it. If he can get you to change your mind by begging, arguing, or whining, he will try to wear you down every time until you finally give in.

Take Action

If he does not obey you when you have told him to wash his hands (within minutes—give him a little slack), then go to him, *say nothing,* take him by the hand, and lead him to the sink. Begin to wash his hands for him, *still saying nothing.* Do not give in to the temptation to scold, fuss, nag, lecture, or hit. Your silence and calm will be *very* effective.

He may squirm to get away. He may cry or scream. Be gentle, but firm. Your *nonverbal* action will reassure him, saying to him, "I mean what I say and I expect you to obey me."

If the child reaches into the cookie jar despite your instructions, quietly and firmly take the cookie jar and place it out of reach. Don't continue to discuss the matter ("It will spoil your appetite." "You heard me."). Continuing to dialogue with your child gives him encouragement and teaches him to be argumentative and obnoxious.

Use Positive Reinforcement

Catch your child being good! Watch for appropriate behavior and give attention, praise, and hugs. Be sure your children know when they have pleased you.

Children want and need attention and will do whatever it

takes to get it. Unfortunately, some of us give more attention to our children when they misbehave.

If two children are eating well at the table and a third is messing up his food or using bad manners, which child will usually get the adult's attention? If we are not careful, we teach children that the quickest way to get us to look at them is to misbehave.

A student of mine who had twin girls, age six, said that she was driving down the interstate one day when Jennie started screaming. Her normal reaction would have been to scream back, "You are going to make me have a wreck. Shut up!" Instead, she began to whisper to Janice, "Where would you like to eat lunch?" Very soon, Jennie stopped screaming to hear what her mother and sister were talking about.

It does not seem natural for us to overlook misbehavior and to give attention to behavior that is appropriate. Rather, it seems almost instinctual to cue into improper actions. ("Ah ha. I caught you!") We have to learn this skill. It takes effort, time, and energy. But it is worth it! The payoff is great!

When/Then

This is one of the easiest and sanest techniques we need to make a part of our repertoire. It is simply using "Grandmother's Rule." "When you have . . . then you may." "When you have put your clothes in the hamper, then I will read you a story," a parent might say to his toddler. "When you have finished your homework, then you can watch television." "When you have the car home on time, then you may use it on Saturday."

The flip side of this technique is, "If you abuse it, you lose it." "If your clothes are not put in the hamper, no story." "If your homework is not completed, no TV." "If you are late—or irresponsible—with the car, you may not borrow it on Saturday."

Make Sure Rules Are Followed

I saw a mother at a neighborhood swimming pool tell her little boy that it would be all right for him to go into the pool just after the lifeguard had blown the whistle and announced that it was time for "Adult Swim." She smiled as he gingerly slipped into the water and swam quietly about, waving to her with a knowing smirk. All the other children were about to have a fit, asking if they could go in, too.

Be Honest in All Things

Our children need for us to be authentic. They can tell when we are not telling the truth—when we say one thing, but feel the opposite.

Little children, even babies, are tuned into the emotions of those around them. That is why they begin to cry an hour before we leave them with a baby-sitter. They sense that we are not at ease with what we are doing.

When parents argue or fight, children get upset and nervous. In fact, research supports the notion that what scares children the most is for their parents to lose control—to yell, scream, and fall apart.

Anger, unhappiness, and frustration are all a part of life. They are as real as their opposites, peace, harmony, and happiness. It is important that we help our children identify, accept, and deal with their own feelings. We can do this in several ways:

• Accept our children's feelings and help them learn to identify them. "I know you are sad, upset, angry." "It is okay for you to be mad, frustrated, unhappy."

- Be there for them. Let them know, "When you are angry, you can cry if you want to. You can also talk about it when you are ready. We are here to help you, to love you, and to offer support when you need it."
- Let your children know that you have been there—that you are not perfect and have had the same kinds of feelings, hurts, disappointments, and failures. Unless we tell them otherwise, they tend to think that we have always been and still are perfect and able to handle frustration calmly and maturely.
- Model honesty. Learn to identify your own feelings in terms of *I messages*. According to Thomas Gordon, author of *Parent Effectiveness Training*, and *Teacher Effectiveness Training*, an I message has three parts: the action, the effect, and the feeling. He suggests that when we recognize that we have a problem (if it is bugging us, it is our problem), then we need to take the responsibility for fixing it. He recommends that we deliver an I message to the other person or persons involved. It is usually helpful to start with, "I have a problem." Then the I message follows: "When you leave your clothes on the floor (the action), someone has to pick them up for you (the effect), and I feel angry (the feeling)." The effectiveness of this message depends on the relationship that exists between you and your child. If there is caring, empathy, sensitivity, and mutual respect, the chances are great that it will not land on deaf ears. The immediate reaction might be silence, disbelief, or shock, but the long-term reaction is often a change in behavior or at least steps in that direction. It might be a new level of dialogue between the two of you, where bargains are struck and new levels of understanding and compromise reached. Learning to deliver I messages helps

us to avoid blaming *you messages*: "You are thoughtless (lazy, ungrateful, sloppy, careless, slow, or stupid)." You messages cripple, invalidate, frighten, label, and often result in defensive behavior by the recipient.

Build the Child's Self-esteem

Each child needs to be recognized for his specialness, his unique qualities, and his gifts. When your child believes in his own potential for good, there is no limit to what he can do with his life. Our children sense how we feel about them and live up to their labels.

If we truly think our child is smart, he will feel smart. If he feels smart, he will become smart.

I challenged an audience one night near Valentine's Day to make an individual valentine for each of their children, writing as many positive traits for each child as they could think of.

Ten years later, after another speech, a father and mother came up to tell me that they had gone home that night and made special valentines for each of their children. They had quickly made them for Child Number One and Child Number Three, but it had taken a while for them to find some positive traits to mention for Child Number Two. Finally, they agreed that she was special because she made people happy, she could always make others laugh. Now, they say, ten years later, her claim to fame is her ability to make others laugh. She has become famous for her puppet shows and is in great demand as an entertainer. They feel certain that she got her start with that valentine many years ago.

Listening/Observing/Caring

Your children know you better than you know them, because they watch, listen, and tune in to you more than you do to them. Our children need us more than we need them. Therefore, in order to survive and cope, they have to know who they are dealing with and what they can count on from us.

We need to become experts on our children. We can only do that when we learn to imitate their behavior of listening, observing, and caring. We are already experts in some areas. We know when there is a change in their behaviors—when they sleep less well or eat less (or more). We often can tell when they are getting sick. We recognize all the signs. Their eyes seem less bright. They are easily frustrated or especially grumpy. If we would talk less and listen and watch more, we could get tuned in to the inner child and learn what makes him tick.

As a graduate student, I was required to write a case study on one child. It was suggested that I choose a child whom I found difficult to like. I had to observe her an hour a day and log her behavior and language. Then I was to interpret both as best I could. By the end of the assignment, I felt differently about the child. I empathized with her point of view, and began to see how she saw life and why she behaved the way she did. I realized that had I been in her shoes, I would have been just like her. It reminded me of the old adage, "If I were you, I would do just as you have done, for I would have your reasons for doing it." By that time, I was so fond of that child, I wanted to adopt her.

We need to learn the skills of passive and active listening. We need to encourage a child to say what he is feeling: "I am mad." Sometimes it helps for us to mirror back to him: "You are angry. I can see that. It is okay. I don't blame you."

Many of us are so anxious to make it right, to shove bad feelings under the rug ("Go to your room until you can wipe that frown off your face and come back smiling."), that we miss out on the wonderful experience of helping our children to accept and cope with their own negative thoughts.

We need to remember that our children have the same kinds of feelings we do. They need to be validated, recognized, appreciated, and respected, just like us. We tend to become careless with their feelings, dishonoring them by joking, being sarcastic, demeaning, and belittling. We pay a high price for such carelessness.

Children who are treated with respect will respect themselves as well as others. Children whose spirits are honored will honor others. They eventually seek out relationships with others who respect and honor them because to do less would be intolerable.

What Parents Can Do to Control Their Child's Environment

Plan Ahead

Often we can prevent problems if we are more careful to anticipate trouble. We can't expect our children to read our minds and behave appropriately if we have not planned ahead.

If we are going to the doctor's office, we know we might have to wait an hour or more. A child without anything to do will find something, and often his inventions may get him or us in trouble.

We cannot expect our child to sit quietly for an hour in church when he does not understand what is going on. In fact, having to do so will most likely set up an adverse reaction to church that may linger for life.

To have a successful shopping trip or dinner out with your child, plan for breaks, diversions, little surprises, child-centered activities, and/or snacks.

For parents who are leaving work and hurrying home for an evening with children, planning ahead might mean a stop for a cup of coffee, a visit with a friend, or a jog around the block. It is well worth the time to build into your life some little enjoyments for yourself. Otherwise, you burn out, become resentful, and your tolerance level is greatly impaired.

Restructure Time

Frequently we get into ruts without realizing it. Mothers say, "The worst time of day is right before supper." Look at those bad times and see what rearrangements can be made. It might help to move suppertime up an hour, or give the child a healthy snack to eat when you first get home. (He may or may not be hungry for dinner later. If not, don't force him to eat. At least he will not become obese or obsessed with food!)

Set the Stage for Compliance

Make it easy for your children to do what is expected of them. Build shelves, footstools, hangers, room dividers, and cubbies. Get them in the habit of putting their possessions away. Teach them that everything has a place where it belongs. At first, it might be necessary to hang reminders around—to provide cues—to help your child get into the habit of putting his possessions away or doing his chores.

A picture of an unhappy dog could be pasted to one side of a piece of cardboard and a picture of a happy dog on the other. As soon as the pet is fed, the happy-faced side is displayed until the next day. If your child needs further reminders, you might have the rule that when the pet is fed, then the child may have her own dinner.

Rearrange the Environment

Sometimes it helps to reassess the arrangement of the room, or rooms. Is it convenient, accessible, livable, comfortable? Can your children reach their clothes easily? Are there shelves for their belongings?

If two children share a room, does each have his or her own private space? Can each have a routine that does not infringe on the rights of the other? Frequently, our children outgrow their spaces before we realize it. By reevaluating from time to time, new needs can be met by making some sensible changes.

Make Substitutions

When our child has demonstrated a need, a new skill, or an interest, it is wise to provide him with an acceptable outlet for practice and development of that skill.

For example, when he bites, give him something on which he can bite. If he wants to color on the wall, give him paper and crayons, and show him where and what he can color.

If he wants to climb, provide safe places for him to climb. If he wants to paint, take him outside and give him a bucket of water and a large brush. Let him paint the side of the house to his heart's content.

If your child gets on a jag saying undesirable words encourage him to go to his room or the bathroom, close his door, and watch himself in the mirror saying those words as often as he wants. Let him know that you don't like to hear them, but he is free to say them out of the earshot of others. (We cannot stop a child from saying anything, but we can teach him where it is acceptable and where it is not.)

Provide a Private Place

Give each child some place to call his own, where no one else can infringe on his freedom, a private place where he can retreat with the assurance that he will be left alone.

Our child needs to know that we have confidence in his ability to pull himself together. It helps if we provide a model for this by retreating ourselves when we need to regroup, think things over, reassess, recover, or simply get away for rest and relaxation. Our child will learn to do the same.

One of my students, whose job was to answer the phone at home during lunch hour for her husband's business, needed to teach her little boys to be quiet while she was on the phone. She devised a plan whereby she would put a certain baseball cap on her head whenever she needed them to be perfectly quiet. She taught them this skill by rewarding them immediately when she was off the phone if they were quiet. They learned to comply beautifully.

One day she saw one of the boys come in the house upset. Later she found him sitting in the big comfortable chair in the den with her baseball hat on. When she approached him, he said that he needed time to be quiet.

Another one of my students has what they call the *snuggly chair*. Whenever anyone sits in it, he or she is letting others know that she/he would like to have a hug, someone to sit with and snuggle up to. She said this overstuffed chair is the favorite chair in the house.

In healthy families, each member is allowed and encouraged to have time to himself where he will not be bothered and where he can have his own thoughts that do not have to be shared with anyone.

State Your Expectations in Advance

Children are usually willing to cooperate when they know ahead of time what to expect. They do not adapt well to changes, disruptions, or sudden interferences. It is only courteous to let them know what is expected of them in time for them to adjust their thinking and accommodate to a different arrangement.

Most of us behave better when we know what is expected of us. If I have planned to spend a comfortable night at home reading by the fireplace, and my husband announces at the last minute that he has invited friends over for dinner, I will have a hard time adjusting. In fact, I might even refuse to fit into his plans. The chances are great that, at best, I will not be happy or agreeable during that evening.

Set Limits

Our children are more secure when they know their limits. Even so, they will probably test them from time to time. They check up on us to see if we will uphold the limits we have set, and actually respect us more when we are consistent.

In time, our children will be able to verbalize and internalize the rules. They will remind each other when someone steps out of line, if you are careful never to allow exceptions.

What Parents Can Do to Help Their Child Learn Self-control

Provide Natural and Logical Consequences

Our children need to learn that all behavior has consequences. In our society, sometimes parents are reluctant to

allow their children to suffer the natural, logical consequences of their actions. Often we don't want our children to
be unhappy or to dislike us. Therefore we try to shield them
from pain. We take their lunches to them if they forget. We
get them another ice cream if they drop their cone. We give
them extra money if they run out. We make their beds if they
don't have time. We finish their homework for them if they
get tired. We buy them another jacket if they lose theirs. We
pay their speeding fine if they get caught.

As long as a child suffers no consequences, he will keep on
trying to break rules, butt in line, slip in without paying, take
what doesn't belong to him, and in short, come to assume
that rules don't apply to him.

We fail to teach our children the realities of life when we
don't allow them to learn from the painful consequences of
their actions. They come to expect others to protect them or
pay for their mistakes. They feel entitled to have whatever
they want. As they get older, some will lie, cheat, or steal to
get what they think should be theirs. Some resort to criminal
behavior. For others, the realities of life become so over-
whelming that they give up and/or lose their enthusiasm for
living. Parents help their child when they allow him to discover the natural consequences of his behavior and learn
from his mistakes.

Develop the Child's Competency, Skills, and Mastery

When our children develop an "I can do" attitude about
life, they like themselves, feel confident, and attract others to
them. Conversely, friends and colleagues are turned off by
those who seem to be helpless and dependent. We do our
children a favor when we encourage their self-reliance and
independence.

When our child can take care of himself and claim many accomplishments, he feels proud and masterful. Success breeds success, so when he sees that he can succeed, he gains energy and enthusiasm for taking more risks and attempting more challenges.

Once after I had been interviewed on television, a cameraman stopped me to ask a question about his child. After we talked, he told me that as a ninth grader, he felt like a misfit—a wimp. His English teacher, who must have sensed his feelings of inadequacy, told him that she wanted him to take charge of all the audiovisual equipment in the classroom that year. At first, he felt that he could not possibly learn how, but then he realized that she must believe he could do it. Therefore he set out to master the challenge. Needless to say, that became the impetus for his life's work. All because of a teacher's faith and belief in him!

The greatest gift we can give our children is a belief in themselves and their ability to make things happen. This ensures them against the feelings of helplessness, despair, and loneliness that are the roots of teenage depression and suicide.

Shape Nonexistent Behaviors

Often we expect too much too soon from our children. In our enthusiasm to shape their behavior, we want to see immediate improvement. A parent might suddenly realize that a neighbor's child who is younger is already picking up his toys or cooking a meal. She might feel that she should expect the same behavior from her child.

If you have ever gone on a fitness kick and decided that you will begin to exercise and go on a diet and cut out coffee, all at the same time, you realize how short-lived and frustrating such a plan can be. Habits are stubborn and hard to break. We need to set up our rewards in a way that will ensure success. In other words, we should be careful to set short-term goals that the child can achieve fairly quickly.

Appendix D includes ideas for setting up incentives to create a win/win situation with your children as you help them break self-defeating habits and develop desired behaviors.

Problem-Solving

One useful tool to teach children is a six-step problem-solving technique:

1. State the problem
2. Brainstorm the alternatives
3. Select one possible solution
4. Implement the solution
5. Reassess the plan
6. Start over, if unsuccessful

Once the technique is learned and understood, it is surprising how even very young children can apply these steps to solve their own problems.

In one family, two sisters, nine and ten, shared a bedroom but began to need privacy. Their brainstorming session produced the following suggestions:

1. Buy another house with more bedrooms.
2. Add another bedroom to the existing house.
3. Make the garage into a bedroom.
4. Stay in the treehouse.
5. Stay in the camper.

6. Divide the room in half, clearly marking each girl's side.
7. Give each girl a private corner of the room.
8. Give each girl a lock box in which to keep personal things such as diaries.
9. Switch rooms with Mom and Dad. Since theirs is larger, the bunk beds could be separated giving each girl their own space.
10. Move the computer table out of girls bedroom and separate the bunk beds.

The first three solutions were ruled out by Mom and Dad for financial reasons, but it was agreed that the camper or treehouse would be okay for an occasional fun night out. Mom and Dad had no desire to give up their room so that solution was dismissed; the family could find no other place in the house for the computer table so that solution was ruled out as well. Dividing the room in half had the potential of creating too many fights so it was eliminated also.

The family decided that the most workable solutions were to allow the girls a locked box for personal possessions as well as a corner of the room for their very own.

After applying the problem-solving techniques and working out a solution of their own, the girls were more respectful of each other's privacy.

Offer Incentives for Appropriate Behavior

When your child is very young, he needs the rules to be simple, clear, and enforced. He feels more secure when he knows exactly what he can count on from the adults in charge. Children cope better when there is a predictable routine—a schedule that stays constant from day to day.

When we find ourselves inconsistently enforcing rules, it is probably wise to reexamine the rules and make sure they are necessary, age-appropriate, and worth our time. If we decide affirmatively, then it helps to have incentives for the child (and maybe for us) to help him develop a new routine.

Children want what they want when they want it. Parents give presents, favors, and/or privileges to children daily. It is wise for us to teach our children to delay gratification and to work for what is important to them.

Unless we are careful, many times we buy presents or give special privileges when we feel good, when we have money in our pockets, or when our children are demanding. In other words, we are inconsistently rewarding them at inappropriate times.

They fail to learn the satisfaction that comes from setting short-term and long-term goals and achieving success through work.

Bad habits are hard to break and good habits are sometimes difficult to establish. We do our children a favor when we teach them that they have control over their own behavior, that they can break self-defeating patterns, and they can replace them with behaviors that will make them proud, productive, and effective.

We can accomplish this by offering incentives for our child's effort to improve his performance.

Most children become excited about their ability to discipline themselves and take great pride in the rewards they earn. They take good care of the possessions they have acquired by steadily working toward a much-wanted goal.

If we want our child to get up with an alarm, we might suggest that he earn a sticker each morning he is successful. When he has five stickers, he can have a quarter to play a video game the next time we go to the shopping mall. (Most of us dish out quarters to our children, anyway. Why not let him earn them?)

When we think our child should be assuming more responsibility for bringing his work home from school, we can give a token for each day he remembers. In order to watch television after dinner, he must have earned his token. When he has ten tokens, he can invite a friend over.

If I am worried because my daughter seldom chooses to read for pleasure, I can suggest that she earn a sticker for every fifteen minutes she reads anything. When she has twelve stickers, we will go the library and let her select another book. When she has thirty stickers, she can get her ears pierced. After that, for every thirty stickers, I will give her one dollar to save toward buying new earrings.

If I am worried because my adolescent's grades have been steadily sliding since I stopped helping with his homework, I can ask him what he is willing to work for. He might want some brand-name tennis shoes. We agree that he earns one point for every fifteen minutes of uninterrupted studying. Thirty points gets him the shoes he wants. (If this is a big problem, you could arrange for him to earn his television time: every fifteen minutes of studying translates into fifteen minutes of watching television.)

As children get older, we should remember that we still have a lot of leverage. We should be careful not give our child everything he wants. He will appreciate his possessions (and eventually, us) more if we teach him the satisfaction of working hard for the pleasures he wants in life.

When Incentives Don't Work/Major Misbehavior

If we have tried an incentive program to break an undesirable habit and replace it with a better habit, and it doesn't work, we can learn some very important lessons.

Obviously, we know that our child's need for that behavior is greater than his need for the reward we offered. Now our job is to look for what is lying beneath the surface of the behavior.

It is possible that our child has too many rewards already or that he knows he can have whatever he wants anyway. He might be testing us to see if we will break down and forget to withhold the privilege.

Or it may be that this child is getting more reward with his misbehavior than he expects to receive without it. For example, he may like to engage the family in worrying about his schoolwork or to hear them arguing about his chores. Children might enjoy engaging their parents in their arguments and seeing whose side their parents will take.

I know of a teenager who refused to earn points for studying even for a much-wanted computer. When his mother talked with him about it later, he confessed that he had hoped that if his grades were bad enough, his parents would turn their anger toward him instead of toward each other. This was his effort to help save their marriage.

It is important for us to take our children's major misbehavior seriously. If it is more than a bad habit that can be broken and replaced by a better habit, we need to try to find the source of the problem.

A child who can express his needs and problems will not be forced to act them out. Therefore we need to employ all the skills available to help our child.

It is important not to punish the symptom of the problem. That is like putting a filling on top of a cavity. The cavity (problem) continues to eat away at the tooth (child), thus causing further decay (more misbehavior/acting out).

Often you can locate the source by talking with and listening to your child. Invite him to engage in dialogue with you, sharing statements such as: "The thing that worries me the most is . . ." "The one thing I wish were different is . . ." "I wish that I could . . ." "I wish my mother would . . ." "I wish I didn't have to . . ." and "What scares me the most is . . ."

Try to create a climate where your child feels free to express his fears, hurts, needs, anxieties, and worries. Share with him some of your negative feelings from times past (when you were his age) and now. Let him know they are normal feelings and a part of everyone's life.

Sometimes when you are at your wits' end, it helps to own up to your frustration. Go to your child's room, sit on the floor quietly, and remain still. When he seems to be in a receptive mood, try a statement such as: "Life is tough, isn't it?" "I feel frustrated about us," "I feel like I'm not a very good parent," "You are really special to me," "I'm worried," "What's going on?" and "On a scale of one to ten, where are you right now?"

After your initial statement, say no more. Wait. If your child says nothing, try another statement in a few minutes. Our presence and undivided attention is reassuring to most children. New avenues of communication are frequently found when we take time to be still together.

If you still can't get your child to open up, try to find someone he trusts (friend, relative, counselor, teacher). Ask that person to help. Frequently, a child will not want to worry you with his problems, feeling that you will be hurt, or have enough to worry about, or will be disappointed to know how he is feeling.

If these efforts fail, seek professional help. There are excellent resources available for every age group and every level of income. If your first counselor is not a good match, try another. Don't give up after one bad experience. It is crucial to find help before the problems become more complicated and/or irreversible.

Always remember that you are the best expert on your child. You know him better and care about him more than anyone else. No one has your history together. That counts for a lot. Your child needs for you never to give up on him!

Chapter Six

Understanding
Your Child

Knowledge of Child Development

Applying positive discipline techniques in the home requires
a great deal of energy, effort, and understanding. First, parents
need to understand child development. There are excellent
books available that explain developmental sequences, what
children are capable of at different ages, and the best ways to
handle problems as they occur and reoccur. The wise parent
will become a student of child behavior just to make sure that
she/he is not expecting too much too soon from the child.

Other parents, support groups, and parent education
classes are a good resource for information and guidance,
reminding us of different approaches to try as our child
outgrows one stage and enters another.

It is important to remember that each child is different and the techniques that work for one child will not always be effective for another. Children in the same family have different personalities, some of which clash more with one parent than another.

Children's needs change as they grow older. Therefore we must frequently reevaluate and reassess to make certain that our child has not outgrown his need for the rules we are still trying to enforce.

One of the most important factors that determines parent effectiveness is authenticity. It is also one of the most difficult concepts to teach and/or assess. Authenticity is the quality that makes us real, worthy of trust, and genuine. Our behavior needs to be congruent, that is, "Say what you mean, and mean what you say." Our body language and verbal language must convey the same message.

Frequently, our attitude gives us away. We can say the same words in ten different ways. For example, I can say "Come here" in a way that makes you curious and willing to come, I can say it in a way that makes you afraid and want to go the other way, or I can say it in a way that is neither compelling nor replusive.

The history of the relationship we have established with each child will determine to a great extent the effectiveness of our discipline. If a parent is nurturing, sensitive, and available, the child may feel freer to test limits than he would with another less available caregiver. The close and trusting relationship between parent and child requires that the parent be especially careful to be consistent and confident in her discipline.

Although the use of fear and physical punishment (inflicting pain for the purpose of hurting) for discipline often get immediate results and bring about instant obedience, I believe that in the long run, they lead to fear and avoidance.

When we treat a child with respect, two positive things happen: the child wants to please us, and the child wants to imitate us. Discipline becomes easier as the child gradually internalizes the rules we place on him and eventually imposes rules on himself.

In other words, our job is to work ourselves out of a job.

Infancy

We are our children's first mirrors, and they look into our faces to see who they are. We are the architects of our child's self-image.

If the child sees the look of disgust, he believes that he is disgusting. If he sees anger, he believes that he is unworthy. If he sees fear, he will be afraid.

On the other hand, if the infant receives the love and nurturing he needs, he will decide that the world is good and can be trusted. He internalizes this belief to mean, "When I express my needs, someone cares and something good happens to me. My needs must be good. Therefore, I must be good."

If the baby doesn't establish a healthy sense of trust, he will either act out, become clingy and demanding, or will withdraw into himself, feeling that he is empty and no good. Extreme deprivation of love may cause the child to become chronically depressed.

Parents and caregivers need to tune themselves in to the needs of the infant, deciphering their different cries and trying to meet the needs when they arise. If they are hungry, feed them; if they are bored, give them attention and stimulation; if they are uncomfortable, give them comfort; if they are tired and sleepy, put them down to rest, even if they fuss.

By the way the infant is touched and held, comforted and

loved, he will begin to define himself. His job is to take in and to receive from others. He is what he is given. The infant thrives because we are there for him and would actually fail to thrive—or die of mourning—without us.

Toddler

As the child becomes a toddler, we must set limits and teach him that there is order in life. He can learn to wait, to delay gratification, to pick up what he drops, to put his things where they belong, and to treat possessions and others with respect.

Of course, at times he will be unhappy and resistant. He will exercise his newly developed language and autonomy with "no" and temper tantrums. We need to be firm and loving, not giving in to his undue demands and following through on what we require of him. Pick him up and take him, if he refuses to walk. Remove him from the group if he hits and hurts others. Take him in the house if he runs into the street. We don't need to carry on a dialogue, reprimand or scold him, or hurt him when he rebels. We should just take over for him until he has regained control and can obey of his own volition.

Model the behaviors that we want our children to emulate. I guarantee, in time, they will come to be like us (in more ways than we want). Your children will grow up and talk like you, walk like you, and have the same manners you have. They might not always choose to behave properly (Do we?), but in time, they will figure out where and when it pays for them to act their best.

It is my hunch that when we get all upset about some small issue such as manners or whether the child eats all his peas, we are actually focusing on an inconsequential matter to avoid facing what is really going on. When I get crazy over something small and insignificant, if I stop and check myself, I soon realize that something of far greater magnitude is bothering me and I don't know how to fix it.

In Tidewater, Virginia, where I live, military families are constantly faced with deployments, three to six-month separations, which temporarily stress the entire family. Parents tell me that right before the impending separation, tempers flare, mishaps occur, and arguments get out of control. It is easier to deal with burned toast than to deal with the doom, devastation, and fear that lie just beneath the surface.

In toddlerhood, the foundation is laid for the rest of life. The child is finding answers to "Who is in charge here?" "What rules do I have to live by?" and "What is expected of me?"

The answers he emerges with are determined by the actions and reactions of those around him. He will do what works. If his caregivers are harsh, punitive, and mean, he will become frightened and withdrawn or demanding and aggressive. If they are inconsistent, he will play one adult against another and exert his energies daily to test the limits. He will feel more secure and live up to what is expected of him more easily if those in charge of him are loving and consistent.

Preschooler

As the child enters his preschool years, he needs to be free to exert his initiative and imagination. He is capable of a great deal of fantasy and often confuses this with fact. We should not accuse him of lying when he makes up stories. His imagination is very vivid and needs to be nourished. It lays the cornerstone for abstract thinking in the adolescent years.

(It makes sense to tell the child that we know he made up the story and encourage him to think up other endings to popular fairy tales and nursery rhymes.)

This is the age when fears are at their highest. The preschooler frequently has a bad dream and thinks it really happened, or sees something scary on TV and has nightmares. Although before he may have been quite content to sleep in a dark room, now he wants the hall light on and the door open. A routine is very important to him, and he may need many reassurances during the night.

We find that this child is now capable of handling more responsibility at home. He can be expected to take better care of his possessions, remember to do his chores, and to internalize simple rules of behaving in small groups of children. He can generalize rules to other authority figures and become very attached to teachers and other adults.

It is imperative that he meet with success in his first school experiences. Since he needs to be able to initiate his own activities, and since he learns through his play by doing and creating, good preschools provide stimulating activities on all levels and allow the child to choose those activities that are appropriate for his level of development.

This child needs to feel good about his own abilities and to feel that he fits and belongs, so a low teacher-pupil ratio is most desirable in the classroom. He needs to feel that people know and care about him and that he can do what is expected of him.

It is the parent's responsibility to ensure that the placement suits the child. We need to find classrooms that fit the child and not try to reshape the child to fit the school. If the child starts off his first academic experiences feeling that there is something wrong with him, his feelings of intellectual inadequacy can last a lifetime.

Middle Years Child

In the middle years, the child will be seeking to establish his sense of industry. He will be developing skills and mastery that he will call upon for the rest of his life, for pleasure as well as for productive work. The parent's job is to provide him with many different role models (who are actively pursuing worthwhile and enjoyable endeavors), so that he can discover his own natural gifts, inclinations, and talents.

I met a woman in Nashville last year who told me that five of their six children had followed their father's footsteps into the medical profession. When they were asked why they had made that choice, they agreed that it was because their father had whistled as he left for work each day. They caught his enthusiasm for his work.

Children during this time can establish excellent work habits. They can learn to set short-term goals and become excited and enthusiastic about striving for them. They take great pride in their accomplishments and build eagerly on their successes.

Fortunately for us, a child of this age still loves to be with his parents. He is not embarrassed to be seen with us in public. If we are not careful, it is easy to take advantage of him. He can easily be pushed aside with "I'm busy," "Can't you ever be quiet?" or "Go away." Since a child this age can be so resourceful, he will oblige and go away, but we will be sorry later. When he is an adolescent and we want him to talk with us, he may reverse the dialogue with, "I'm busy," "Can't you ever stop asking questions?" or "Go away."

Children between the ages of six and twelve can be so reliable that there is a tendency in some families to place too much responsibility on their shoulders, to put them in charge of younger children, leave them home alone, give them too many chores to do, and/or expect them to meet our emotional needs.

Some parents use them as their sounding boards, confiding in them and seeking their advice on adult matters. Although they may seem to feel honored to be trusted, such responsibility can become a heavy burden for a child. It can keep him from forming attachments to his peers and learning many of the important lessons of childhood. Years later, he may realize that he was never allowed to be a child. At that time, he may suddenly revert to childishness, disregarding his adult responsibilities and walking away from jobs and people who are counting on him.

If a child does not develop a healthy sense of industry, mastering skills, he will develop a feeling of inadequacy or laziness. He may become an emotional cripple, feeling incapable and expecting others to do for him what he should and could be doing for himself.

Adolescence

As a child enters his teen years, we hope he has a well-developed sense of trust, autonomy, initiative, and industry, for he will need them to embark on the journey of adolescence. This will be the time he needs to establish his identity. At some level, he realizes that the goal is independence and separation from those who have taught and nurtured him to this point.

It is a scary time. He will be trying on many hats, experimenting with different roles, establishing ties with some who are like him and some who are different. He will be looking to other adults whom he can trust. He will be sharing family secrets with significant others. He will no longer want to let his parents know everything he is thinking or doing. He will need to form ties outside the family, but still feel the safety and assurance that comes from a secure support system at home.

He needs to know that his parents understand what is going on with him and can allow and applaud his growing independence and need for privacy.

This is a time when parents need to have their own lives in order and not derive their own self-esteem from their children. If we are counting on our adolescents for company, solace, understanding, or appreciation, we are in for a big letdown. This is a time when the teenager needs to be allowed to take some risks, knowing that at home his parents will continue to be there for him and help him learn from his mistakes. He needs for us to see the potential adult within and gradually to treat him more like the mature person he is striving to become.

Chapter Seven

Launching Your Child: From Theory to Practice

Our job then, as parents, is to work ourselves out of a job. We must get our children to the place where they can live without us. (Of course, conversely, we also need to get ourselves ready to live without them. I was never prepared for how hard this would be. I wish that I had been told to prepare myself for this.)

By the time a child is twelve, she needs to be able to make good decisions on her own behalf. She needs to know how to take care of her body and her possessions and to make good use of her time and energy. She needs to know how to use her mind to weigh alternatives, to anticipate conse-quences, and make decisions based on what will be best for her future.

This is not to say that our children will be leaving home when they are twelve, but it is to say that by this time, in our scary society, they need to be able to say no to the negative but powerful and enticing influences that are so available in our transient and violent world.

The way we help our children become good decision-makers is to start when they are young, giving them choices whenever possible, and as they grow older, giving them more and more opportunities to discover the consequences of their decisions.

Sylvia B. Rimm, Ph.D., in her book, *How to Parent So Children Will Learn,* suggests that we should give choices to children in a V of love. The sides of the V represent the boundaries that we provide for them as they grow and learn. If we do our job well, by the time our child is in high school, she will be able to make almost all of her own decisions.

Dr. Rimm reminds us that children want more and more power as they grow older. This is natural. The difficulty comes when we give children too much control too early. It is very hard, if not virtually impossible, to take back control, once it is given. Therefore we must give it carefully, in small increments, aiming for adolescence as the time when a young person will be in charge of much of her own life.

One of the biggest mistakes parents are making in today's world is to give little children too much power too soon. One of the disastrous results is that by the time a child is an adolescent, she has become so powerful that her parents feel powerless and resentful, realizing that they have lost control and their child has no respect for them. These parents can hardly wait for their children to leave home!

We want our children to start early, realizing that they have good heads on their shoulders and that we have faith in their ability to make wise decisions on their own behalf. Furthermore, we respect their ability to think and their right to decide what is best for them.

We need to realize that there are several areas of our child's life that belong to him and should be left in his domain. In other words, there are certain things we *cannot* make a child do. We cannot make a child like or dislike another person. We cannot make him eat, sleep, learn, talk, go to the potty, or stop sucking his thumb. We are wasting our time and energy getting involved in battles such as these. Furthermore, we run the risk of making the problem bigger. The child can now direct his energies toward the power struggle instead of toward using his mind to decide what is in his best interests.

One more reminder is that all children and all parents are different. Therefore, no technique will work for all children or for all parents. Each parent needs to feel that what he chooses to do fits him and his set of values. A technique that may work for one child may not work for another child. Therefore, we have to keep trying until we find what works.

The important questions for us to always ask ourselves when trying a new technique are:

- Am I honoring my child's spirit?
- Am I giving him as much freedom as he can handle?
- Am I helping him to believe in his ability to think, figure things out, and make choices?
- Am I gradually turning the control of his life over to him?
- Am I being true to myself?

The following are suggestions for handling the common problems that face all families.

Biting

Biting is one of the problems which concerns parents of young children the most. Some helpful tips are:

1. NEVER play-bite with your child, or laugh when he bites. He will think this is a game.
2. NEVER bite your child back. He will think this behavior is acceptable. (Adults must always model mature behavior.)
3. REMOVE the "biter" from the "bitee," and from other children. Put him in a safe place, i.e., a playpen (the SAME place each time this incident occurs).
4. CONSOLE the child who was bitten. Hug, hold, comfort.
5. WAIT until the biter has settled down before you talk with him. AFTER he has gotten quiet—no matter how long it takes—invite him to rejoin the group, asking him if he is ready to play without biting.
6. If this incident is repeated, do EXACTLY the same thing again—and again—and again.
7. If you are in a group setting, and this behavior continues over a matter of weeks, the parents will have to be notified that the child must lose the privilege of attendance for a short while.
8. If the behavior persists or gets worse, professional help is warranted—to see what frustrations exist in the child's life which might provoke such outbursts.

Tattling

When a child comes to us to "tell on" another child, he *needs* several things:

1. to know that you hear him;
2. to know that you care;
3. to know what to do about it.

He may *want* something else: to get someone else in trouble.

We must remember that we want our children to come to us when they have a problem, instead of slugging it out. Therefore, we cannot afford to send them away or shame them for coming, with "No tattling," or "I don't want to hear it."

We can address his "need" with:

1. "I'm sorry."
2. "I'm sorry your ears had to hear that." (If he is telling you about another child's bad language.)
3. "Thank you for telling me."
4. "I would never do that to you."
5. "That must have made you angry."
6. "I imagine that hurt your feelings."
7. "Why don't you tell Susan how that made you feel."
8. "Do you think you and Susan can work it out?"
9. As a last resort, if the child is still not satisfied or willing to resume his work or play, we can say, "I'll take care of it." Then we can dismiss him.

The important issue here is that we don't want him to learn that his effort did, in fact, get another child in trouble.

If we feel that intervention is needed, we make it our business to become more observant and catch the other child misbehaving. ("Susan, I saw you tear Alicia's paper. We need to talk.") OR, if the situation has already occurred, we might ask her, "What is going on?" In all likelihood, Susan will tell on herself, or at least give a version of the story that will give you important insights, which you can use to solve the problem.

Complaining

Children need to be able to express their feelings. We need to realize that they are entitled to feel what they feel and want what they want. WE SHOULD NOT TAKE IT PERSONALLY when children are unhappy. Rather we need to learn to VALIDATE their feelings—NOT try to talk them out of them.

- "Ginny hit me. I hate her." ("You are angry with Ginny.")
- "My cereal is soggy. I don't want anymore." ("You are finished eating your cereal. You don't like it when it gets soggy.")
- "I want a candy bar." ("I can understand why you would want a candy bar. That would taste good.")
- "I want to stay home today." ("You would like not to have to go to school.")
- "It's not fair that I have to pick up the toys. She played with them, too." ("You don't think it's fair that you have to clean up.")
- "Johnny says he doesn't like me. He won't let me play." ("I can imagine that would hurt your feelings.")

Many times the child will continue to express feelings— which will be healing for her. After we have validated—and when she is finished expressing—then we move on. We give a choice about what is done next. ("Do you want to walk or be carried to bed?" "Which pants would you like to wear to school?")

Allowances

It is important for children to understand the value of money. By the time they leave us, they need to be able to budget, save, and spend wisely. Therefore, we need to get started early letting children gain experience by making choices when they are young.

As soon as a child understands the value of a nickel, a dime, and a quarter, he might be given a small allowance. With this money, he can be given the opportunity to save some and to choose how to spend the rest.

As the child grows older, his allowance should increase to include more and more of his expenses. For example, he can be told that he will receive a certain amount of money, and with his money, he will be expected to purchase things such as school lunches, notebook paper, and extra drinks.

By the time a child is an adolescent, it is wise to give him a clothing allowance, as well. When he understands that this money will not be subsidized, he will be more willing to choose carefully by looking for bargains, sales, and specials when making choices for his wardrobe.

As we think of the V of love, we will realize that when the child is young, we may want to limit his choices in the store to ones we think are suitable. By letting him know that we honor his wishes and tastes, we give him opportunities to stretch his brain and live with the consequences of his actions (i.e., all of his money is spent and he will have to live with the frustration of waiting for the next allotment).

We have to be willing to let our children struggle and suffer with disappointment over bad choices, missed opportunities, and empty wallets. Sometimes the best way to learn is through our mistakes.

Being on Time

We want our children to grow up to be responsible human beings. We must start early letting them live with the consequences of being late before they will learn how to put forth the effort that it takes to be on time.

"Helicopter parents" make excuses for their children, rescue them from the consequences of putting off their chores, homework, thank-you notes, and meeting their obligations.

Conscious parents remain friendly but state the facts when addressing this problem. "If you are late to school, you will probably get detention, and you will have to figure out a way to get home." "As soon as your chores are done, you are free to make plans for the weekend." "When your thank-you notes are written, you can go out to play."

It is important that you *not* remind, scold, threaten, or rescue. Hang tough. Remember your goal—a responsible child.

Staying in Bed at Night

It is amazing how many hours are spent in the average household trying to get children to stay in their beds at night. It is sad to see the power that some parents give to their children when it comes to going to bed and staying there.

Children need their sleep and parents need their privacy.

Children also need to know that their own bed is comfortable and a safe place to be.

Some families enjoy "the family bed" and encourage their children to sleep with them as long as they wish. This is certainly a decision that parents are free to make. For them, bedtime is probably not a problem.

However, there are many parents who really want their children to sleep in their own beds in the nice rooms which they have provided for them. It is for these parents that the following suggestions are made.

- Remember that you can't *make* a child sleep. Any energy expended by you in this effort will be wasted.
- You do have control over your own actions, such as, what you do when the child cries, when you go to his room, when and what you say to him, whether or not you allow him in your bed, and how you interact with him.
- It is important to decide, as parents, what you feel is the best policy for your family. Will children never be allowed in your bed? Will they be allowed only when they are sick? Will they be allowed only after the sun comes up in the morning? Will they be allowed one night a week? Once you make this decision (hopefully before you have children), then you are well on your way. The trouble with most parents is that they have never discussed the matter, and when the problem presents itself (the child is crying and you are sleepy), they take the line of least resistance and put the child in the parents' bed. Then the problem has begun.

If your children are not allowed in their parents' bed, you may need support to follow through and be consistent. Here are some strategies that may help.

Babies need to get used to going to bed awake. It is a good policy to help them get calm by rocking or feeding them, but to put them in bed *awake*. This way they will get the notion that you trust them to be able to put themselves to sleep. They will come to feel comfortable and to enjoy their bed.

Once you have decided that the baby's need is to sleep, leave him in his room until he is asleep. When he wakes up and cries, go into his room and pat him on his back, saying nothing, if you think he needs more sleep (i.e., in the middle of the night). Do not pick him up or sing and talk to him, for he will concude that it is time to visit. After he has settled back down, leave the room and don't go back until he has gone back to sleep. The reasons that I suggest for you to go to his room whenever he cries are twofold: one, he needs to know that you are still nearby, and second, you need to be sure that he is all right (no arm between the crib slats, no illness).

When the child is older, bedtime usually becomes a problem. It is very natural for children to resist leaving the family and going off to their room to be by themselves.

Who should decide when it is time to go to bed? Bedtime is determined by what time you, the parents, decide is best, based on how much rest and quiet time you think the child needs and how much rest and private time you need.

The child will have control over many decisions surrounding the bedtime, i.e., whether or not the light is left on, whether or not he listens to music (low enough not to be heard by others), whether or not he plays or looks at books quietly, whether or not he goes to the bathroom or gets a drink of water, and whether or not he sleeps.

The parents have control over whether or not they interact with the child (talk to him) for any reason after the established bedtime. They might announce, when they have concluded the nightly ritual, "I will look forward to seeing and being with you in the morning. I hope you have an enjoyable and restful night."

When children are treated in this manner, they get the notion early that their parents trust them to make good decisions about their sleep. If they choose to stay up too late, they will be exhausted the next day. They may fall asleep in school or need a nap in the afternoon, missing out on playtime. We need to be prepared for the fact that our children will make some unfortunate choices. We all have to know how it feels to be too tired to enjoy the day before we commit to going to bed at a reasonable hour.

Children treated in this manner will also learn to respect their parents' space and privacy. In the long run, family members will enjoy each other more when they have some time apart.

For more on this, see page 130.

Potty Training

We cannot make a child use the potty. The more power struggles we engage in, the longer it will be before he masters this skill and takes on the responsibility for keeping himself dry.

We need to make sure that the child is ready to be potty trained. There are three stages through which a child must go before he is ready to be trained:

1. The child knows he has wet. (He announces that his diapers are wet or soiled.)

2. The child knows that he is wetting. (He announces that he is "doing it" right now!)
3. The child knows that he needs to wet. (He announces that he needs to "do it.")

We need to wait for Stage 3 before considering potty training. When we know that he can *anticipate* the need to use the potty, we introduce him to the potty and to "big boy pants." We let him know that whenever he would like to use the potty, then he will be able to wear big boy pants. You might take him shopping and let him choose his favorite kind.

From now on, when it is time to get dressed, you ask him which he wants—diapers or big boy pants. You let him know that if his choice is big boy pants, then you will expect him to use the potty.

Of course, meanwhile, you are giving him ample opportunities to see others use the potty, so this will seem like a natural thing to do.

If he should have an accident in his big boy pants, you act as nonchalant as possible, saying, "Oops, I guess you forgot. We'll need to put the diapers back on now." The next time you dress him, you ask again which he prefers.

If he seems totally disinterested in using the potty, you probably should go back to diapers and wait until he shows more interest.

Sometimes, it helps to put a chart up in the bathroom, and let him put a sticker on the chart or underwear on the little bears you have drawn on a poster (see more about this on page 128), every time he has a success in the potty. When all the bears have their underwear, we call Grandma and tell her!

Sometimes it is a good idea to let him decide at what point he would like to stop wearing diapers. For instance, you might ask if he thinks his third birthday would be a good time to start wearing big boy pants. Often it helps to announce ahead of time what is going to happen on a special day. Then everyone talks about it and tells the baby-sitter so that the child commits to the plan in his head before he physically commits to the transition for real.

When problems arise around toilet training, such as accidents and/or constipation, it is absolutely essential that we back off. We need to let the child know that we have faith in his ability to handle this responsibility, and he can just let you know how you can help. Then, act like it doesn't matter to you. Shrug your shoulders when there is an accident. You might leave the "pull-ups" on a bottom shelf where he can get them himself. You might leave rags and towels where he can reach them for "spills."

When a child realizes that his power over toileting doesn't upset you, he will be much more likely to assume responsibility for this part of his life.

Eating Problems

Children are born with the ability to know when they are hungry and when they are full. They stop eating when they have had enough. Our job is to provide them with healthy choices and honor the part of them that regulates the amount they eat. This is easier said than done.

For many reasons, somewhere along the way, many children get the notion that they eat to please us. Some of the ways we convey this idea to them are:

• By coaxing them to eat when they obviously have lost interest

- By telling them that they can't have "this" until they have eaten "that"
- By becoming a policeman over their food
- By paying too much attention to what and how much they eat
- By "tricking" them into eating (the old zooming airplane routine)
- By implying that if they love us, they will eat what we have prepared for them
- By offering food in place of comfort, at times when the child is angry, upset, tired, scared, bored, or lonely.

Rudolph Dreikurs, in *Children, the Challenge,* says, "Eating problems are caused by misbehaving parents." By this he means that parents get too involved in the child's eating habits and force the child to lose his ability to regulate himself. Following are some tips for parents who have "misbehaved."

Provide healthy food for your family.

Be a model for healthy eating yourself. This might be the hardest assignment yet; however, it is imperative. If we want our children to make good choices, they must see us doing the same. If we talk about which foods are good for us, make us feel good, are low in fat, give us energy, and how much we enjoy eating them, then our children will pick up our attitudes.

Allow the child to choose from healthy alternatives such as fruit, yogurt, vegetables, and bread, whenever he is hungry. Let him "graze," or eat five or six times a day, as he feels the need.

If you want your family to enjoy mealtime together, announce that no snacks are allowed an hour before dinner. Serve the food family style, and let the child choose which foods he wants and how much. Act unconcerned if he chooses not to eat anything. Let him know that you enjoy that food and will be able to take it for lunch the next day if he doesn't care for it.

Make the conversation at mealtime pleasant. Talk about events of the day. Encourage each family member to tell something fun they did, something new they learned, the nicest thing that happened to them, or their favorite part of the day.

Don't mention food, unless it is to say how much you are enjoying it. Don't focus on problems such as table manners—your children will imitate yours.

When a child is restless, loses interest in eating, argues, or fusses, give him the choice of going to his room or playing quietly in the den. Help him down if he is in the high chair.

From the very beginning, you want to make mealtime a privilege and an enjoyable occasion. Anyone who keeps this from happening may leave.

Convince children that their tummies belong to them. They have the good sense to know when they are hungry and when they are not. They also have the good sense to know what foods work best for them. Realize that they, like the rest of us, will have to learn some lessons the hard way. Which of us has not, from time to time, felt miserable from overeating? It is at such times that we vow to be more careful the next time we are invited to an all-you-can-eat.

Children are born with the ability to know when they are hungry and when they are full. They stop eating when they have had enough. Our job is to provide them with healthy choices and honor that part of them which regulates the amount they eat.

Thumb-Sucking

A child's thumb (and fingers) belong to him. If he wants to suck them, he will. Many babies suck pacifiers. Others suck their thumbs. Actually, both provide comfort and tend to calm and soothe.

As a child develops his capacity for frustration and his interest in the world around him, his need for sucking diminishes. Most of the time, his interest in his thumb or pacifier gradually decreases until it is gone. Some children stop sucking on their own. Others suck only when they are tired or going to sleep. A pacifier can be thrown away while a thumb cannot.

If you decide that your child is ready to give up his pacifier, it is good to announce ahead of time that on a certain day (i.e., his third birthday), he will be old enough to throw it away. You can talk about it a lot with him, so that he can start convincing himself that he will be able to accomplish this. On his third birthday, you can make a big deal over this passage. You might let him select the time and place for disposing of the pacifier. (It is *not* a good idea to get him to give it to a smaller sibling. He will probably try to take it back, and/or be jealous of the little one who now has what used to belong to him.)

It is not that easy to get rid of thumb-sucking. I have found that the more it is talked about, both in front of the child and within his earshot, the longer the problem persists.

Here, as in other matters, the trick is to convince the child that within him lies the capacity to stop sucking his thumb *when he is ready*. Let him know that when he wants to stop, you will be more than happy to help him by offering an incentive chart. When he expresses a desire for something that he does not need and that you are not inclined to buy for him, tell him that you will help him work for it. Whenever he goes one-third of the day without sucking his thumb, he can put a sticker on the chart (or a ring on one of the ten fingers you have drawn on a chart). When he has collected ten, he can get a dollar, and when he has enough money, you will go with him to buy something that he has been wanting.

Trust that your child will one day *want* to stop sucking his thumb (peers usually help this to happen), and when he does, you will be there to help.

Chores

It is important for children to know early on that they belong to a unit—a family—a workforce that has common interests and goals. This unique arrangement of people (the family) has a lot going for it. The members love and care about each other. They are committed to one another and they feel safe when they are together. Their common goal is shared responsibility—that of making everyone a contributing member. As each family is able, he does his part for the common good of all.

In other words, as they are able, all family members take responsibility for getting the work done. Some contribute money, others contribute their time and energy. It is necessary for each person to have jobs to do—jobs that are important and that no one else will do for them.

Little children can be taught to put their clothes in the hamper when they take them off, to hang their towels on the rack after a bath, to wash the sink with a sponge when they spit into it, and to throw the tissue into the trash after they have used it. This can be taught with a simple when/ then—"When you have put your clothes in the hamper, I will read you a story." Soon the child automatically puts his clothes in the hamper when he takes them off, instead of throwing them on the floor.

As children get older, they need to be given more responsibility. It is always advantageous to let them have some imput as to the division of labor. Perhaps a list can be made of the chores that must be done in a week. Together, the family (or the children, if they are old enough) can assign "weights" to the different chores, according to their level of difficulty. They can divide the number of participating people into the total, and divide the chores evenly.

It might be wise to have a family meeting once a week or once a month to reassign chores.

Children can have some power over when they do the chores, how they do the chores (as long as they pass inspection), if they help each other, and maybe even if they pay someone else to do the chores. However, there are certain guidelines that are nonnegotiable.

In order to have weekend privileges (or TV or telephone or car privileges), chores must be done by noon on Saturday.

Complaining or grousing about chores will be ignored by parents. It is important that we spend some time teaching our child how to do the chore. At first, it might be wise to let him work with you as he is learning. Then, as he becomes more independent, suggest that he call you to come see when he is satisfied with the job.

It is important not to pay money for chores (unless you are paying another family member to do them for you out of your allowance).

It is important that chores be interesting, not just boring tasks. (Planting flowers in the garden is much more interesting than weeding it.)

It is important that no one ever comes behind and redoes

a job for another person, or that a parent feels sorry for a child and does his chore for him because the child is tired or busy.

In order for a child to feel like a contributing member of the family, it is absolutely essential that he be expected to handle his work assignments responsibly. One of the by-products of this way of handling chores will be that your child will work harder to keep the house clean and orderly, knowing the amount of energy it takes to get it that way.

Car Privileges

A child should not be allowed to drive the car until he has shown that he can be trusted to behave responsibly. Just because he is fifteen years and eight months does not mean that it is his right to get his learner's permit.

As soon as your child starts talking about driving the car, let him know that before you would even consider it, he must prove to you that he handles other decisions in a responsible manner. Then hang tough. Do not weaken. He cannot get his learner's permit without your signature.

When your child does get his driver's license, let him know that permission to drive will still only be granted by you when you are convinced that he drives responsibly and can be counted on to go where he says he is going and comes back when he says he is coming back.

If he should happen to slip and behave in a way that you consider to be unsafe, or if he cannot be held accountable, the privilege of driving is suspended for a certain amount of time (the length of which has been stated before the privilege was granted). This way, your child knows ahead of time what the consequences of irresponsibility are, and therefore to drive or not to drive is his choice.

Children who are old enough to drive are old enough to make money for gas and insurance. Very few children can make enough money to buy a car. Until such a time, they will be compelled to live by the rules of those who own the car.

Shopping (with a young child)

Some children cannot handle the confusion of a shopping trip. These children should be left home with a sitter, a family member, or a neighbor (whose older child you take with you, as a trade).

When you decide to take your child shopping with you, preparation is necessary.

You should let your child know exactly what he can expect to happen. "We are going to three stores. You will be able to select one package of gum and one drink while we are shopping. You will be able to decide where and when you get them."

You should take him *after* a nap, not when he is tired.

You should take him when *you* are rested, not when *you* are tired.

You should take along something for both of you to eat (a healthy snack or two).

You should plan for some small diversions or rewards during the trip. (Alternate letting him walk and ride in the cart.)

You should take some toys, books, crayons, or games with you and pull them out when he starts getting bored.

You should involve him in the shopping trip, if at all

possible. Let him count people with sneakers on their feet, look for red boxes, select the bananas.

Give your child something to look forward to. "When we finish shopping, if you have chosen to be helpful, we will stop at the park or to get a drink."

If things get totally out of hand, stop the shopping trip. Go to the car and, if necessary, take the child home. Let the child know that the next time you need to go shopping, you will leave him with a sitter. Be sure to follow through. Then wait a few weeks before trying him at the grocery store again.

More suggestions for peace in the grocery store are listed in Appendix C.

Friends

All of us choose friends with whom we feel comfortable, whose traits we admire, whom we find fascinating, or whom we would like to emulate. Therefore, when children choose friends, they have their reasons for making these selections. The more we try to talk them out of their choices, the more we will drive them to those whom we do not like.

I know two ways to help children become more realistic about people with whom they like to be associated.

Engage in conversations about the qualities of people whom you admire. Ask your child to describe a good friend. Suggest that she list those traits that she likes and those she doesn't like in each of her friends. Share some of your concerns about your own friends, saying what you admire and don't admire about them. Don't judge her friends or give your opinion. Let her know that you are very interested in meeting people who are important to her.

Invite her friends to your home. Take them on trips with you. The chances are very great that once your child senses that you are not going to try to restrict her association with her friend, her vision will clear and she will be more able to see the negative traits that seem so glaring to you. It rarely works for parents to forbid their children to see one of their friends. Usually this only serves to make that person more attractive through your children's jaundiced eyes.

Homework

Homework is the child's responsibility. Just as school is his "job," so homework is part of his "job description."

If a parent does homework for his child, he robs the child of the satisfaction of doing it for himself. He also is misleading the teacher into thinking that the child understands the material and can do the work. Furthermore, he is conveying to the child the message that "You can't do your homework yourself; you need me to help you."

Our goal, as conscious parents, is to help our children use their brains to make good decisions on their own behalf. They need to learn how it feels to go to school unprepared, to incur the teacher's wrath, and to face the consequences. Only when they decide that they want to avoid these consequences will they be willing to put forth the effort it takes to set aside time and energy to get the assignments done.

There are many ways parents can help.

- Block out a period of time when the child is expected to set aside other interests (TV, outside play, phone) to read and/ or study.

- Provide a quiet and pleasant place.
- Turn off the TV so that other family members aren't causing a distraction.
- Be a role model for reading, learning, and studying.
- Reinforce what the child is studying by showing an interest in what he has learned. Extend his learning, if possible, with first-hand experiences, field trips, and discussions.
- Offer to help by calling out questions or spelling words, if the child asks.
- Show an interest in the work that he brings home.
- Get to know his teachers, the school itself, other parents, and the school rules. Join the PTA and attend the meetings. Second only to the influence of parents and grandparents in a child's life will be the influence of his teachers.

As your child goes to school, his experiences will broaden, and his success there will be largely dependent upon the bridges you are able to build with his academic world. These bridges are comprised of firm connections, relationships, and reciprocal support. A loving and validating home ensures maximum school success, and satifying school experiences enrich the child's life with his family.

Whining

If we were deaf, children would not whine. They whine because it gets them what they want—our attention.

There is only one way to stop whining. That is to stop giving attention to it. This is easier said than done.

When we say to a child, "Stop whining," that is attention. When we say, "Talk politely, and I will listen," that is attention.

When we say, "If you don't stop whining, I will send you to your room," that is attention. When we say, "What did I say about whining?" that is attention.

The only way we can stop giving attention to whining is to ignore it. That means that when the child whines, we pretend that we are deaf. We do not look, frown, act annoyed, remind, or fuss. We continue whatever we were doing.

The child will whine more, will get louder, might get right in our face. We still ignore it. We keep right on with whatever we're doing—looking at TV, scraping the carrots, talking on the phone (we might have to move into the closet), or eating dinner.

As soon as the child talks in an acceptable tone of voice, you stop what you are doing, look at the child, smile, and respond to whatever she is requesting. "No, I'm sorry, you can't go outside now. You certainly may go as soon as you have picked up your toys."

If she starts whining again, repeat this procedure.

It is a good idea to announce ahead of time that you have changed your mind about whining. From now on, instead of getting mad when she whines, you are going to pretend that you have earmuffs on. You are going to pretend that you cannot hear. As soon as she talks the way she is supposed to, you will promise to stop and respond to what she is saying. It is best to have this conversation at a time when you feel good, perhaps at her bedtime. Be prepared for her to not take you seriously, and be prepared for the whining to increase before it decreases. She will need to test you to see if you are really going to be able to shut your ears to whining.

Pets

Many families decide that having a pet is a good idea. The parents see it as a time to teach the child the responsibility of caring for something other than himself, and the child sees it as a companion for play and comfort.

Even if the rules are discussed ahead of time concerning who will take care of the pet, a child cannot possibly know all that is involved. Therefore, it is imperative to decide whose job it will be to feed, water, walk, and bathe the pet.

If the parents are willing to assume responsibility for pet care, they should not hassle the children every now and then about whose job this is. They may ask for help from time to time, but if they have not made it clear (and stuck by it), they should not engage in guilt trips or shame games.

However, if the children are to be held accountable, guidelines are necessary:

- As soon as the pet is fed, the child may have his dinner.
- As soon as the pet is watered, the child may go out to play.
- As soon as the pet is walked, the child may watch TV.
- As long as the pet is fed, watered, and walked each day, we will keep the pet.
- If there are arguments, slipups, and/or pet neglect, the animal will be sold or given away. Maybe at a later time, your children might be more willing to meet the obligations that accompany pet ownership.

If you find that it makes you too anxious to hear your pet crying for food and/or water, or it makes you too mad at your child, you might decide to change the rules. You may have fallen in love with this animal too much to get rid of it. You can renegotiate and tell your child that you have decided that he is not ready for this responsibility and you are unwilling to let the pet go. Therefore you are going to take on the job yourself for a year, after which you will all revisit the matter.

The main thing to avoid is saying that the job is that of the children, while in reality, you are doing it for them. This sends out many conflicting messages, the most damaging of which are, "You don't have to listen to us. We don't mean what we say. We would rather do the work ourselves than help you become a responsibile human being."

Cleaning the Child's Room

Families differ in their expectations concerning the cleanliness of children's rooms. Some are content to leave it up to the child. It is his room. If he wants to live in a pigsty, that is his business. You can keep the door shut.

Other parents feel that the house belongs to them and they have the right to require that each child keep his room up to a certain standard. They rigidly enforce this rule.

Most families are somewhere in between. Many would like for the child's room to be clean and for him to want to keep it that way. Some fuss often, but give in on occasion, and clean the room themselves, when they can no longer stand the scene.

Conscious parents decide what they want. Perhaps some family problem-solving and brainstorming might help these families to come up with a workable plan. It might take several weeks to iron the kinks out and discover an arrangement that makes sense.

When children are little, they need the task broken down into several specific and measurable portions. They also need lessons. It might be wise to have five areas of the room for which the child is responsible: drawers pushed in, no clothes on the floor, bed made, trash can emptied, no food or food containers in the room. The child can put a check beside the picture of each job that has been drawn on a posterboard. When all five checks are made, he may turn on the TV.

When the child is older, the bargain can be renegotiated, with his input considered. Perhaps the arrangement might be that as soon as his room is cleaned (on Friday), he will be free to make weekend plans (use the phone, play Nintendo, or have a friend over).

Here again, it is important that no one go behind the child to redo his job or to do the job for him. This would be the fastest way in the world to undo all the good that has been done and show him that you don't trust him to do what is expected of him.

Sibling Rivalry

One of the biggest complaints that parents have is the problem of sibling rivalry. Parents ask, "How can two children raised in the same home be so different?" "Do my children really hate each other?" and "Why do they fight so much?"

Sibling quibbling is especially hard for a parent who was himself an only child. The bickering and nitpicking drives him nuts. It is more tolerable for parents who grew up with siblings and can still remember how the fights bugged their parents.

Some facts help us to understand sibling rivalry and some basic principles help us to learn how to minimize it, so that it no longer drives us crazy.

It is unnatural for siblings to rejoice when a new sibling joins the family. This would be just as unlikely as it would be for me to be happy if my husband were to decide to bring another wife home. Even though he might try to convince me that he has plenty of love in his heart for both of us and that we are both nice women and should enjoy each other's company, there is no way that I would willingly accept the intruder.

There is no question about it—there is not as much time or love to go around, now that it must be divided in more parts. A child can certainly figure that out in a hurry. It doesn't feel good to him. Feelings of jealousy are normal.

Children still need one-on-one time with each adult. Wise parents build in such times for each child daily, if at all possible. During this time, much effort is spent trying to get the child to express his fears, wishes, worries, and anger. Bedtime often lends itself to such closeness and sharing.

Having siblings is a wonderful opportunity for children to learn many of the necessary lessons in life. For example, they can learn to give and take, lead and follow, win and lose, love and hate, be mad and forgive, sacrifice and really care for the well-being of another person.

When parents get involved in sibling quibbling, the problems get bigger. When parents stay out of sibling quibbling, children learn to solve their own problems, and the problems diminish. Therefore, when children are arguing, withdraw— either physically (by going to another room) or mentally (by humming, listening to the radio, or making mental grocery lists). Pretend that you are deaf. If you are worried about the physical safety of either child or if you can't withdraw (your makeup is such that for you it is an impossibility), separate the children firmly and quietly. Let them know that they need to go to different rooms and stay there until they feel they can work out their differences. Develop a signal (motioning with your finger) that means, "Okay, you guys, split. Come back when you can work things out."

Be sure, from the very beginning, that you convey to your children that life is not fair, that what is right for one child is not necessarily right for another, that just beause one child needs something new, does not mean that another child needs anything. Don't try to even things out. It will never work, and it will set you up to be the bad guy whenever a child is jealous of a sibling. Sometimes it is a good idea to let children draw straws for who is going to be the one to cut the cake and get the last piece.

Older children should have more privileges. Remember, we are giving more freedom as they develop and mature. Older children should be allowed to stay up later, get a bigger allowance, and make more decisions.

When children argue over the same things a lot, it is time for a family council and some creative problem-solving. Whether it is the TV or who rides where in the car, invite as many solutions to the problem as can be imagined. Let the children know that as long as they work out an agreeable arrangement, you will live by their decisions. However, when you hear quarreling, that will tell you that they need you to make the rules. Then you state your rule: On every even day, Sally rides up front and Ross holds the remote control. On odd days, the privileges are reversed. Of course, if there are more children, a chart for sibling order is posted on the refrigerator (see more about this on page 134).

Some families like the family rule: "If I don't hear the quibbling, you can arbitrate any way you choose. If it lands on my ears, then I will know that you need a time to retreat to your rooms and cool off from being together." Of course, when they try to get you to take sides, you remind them of the above rule.

Temper Tantrums

Most children discover temper tantrums when they are about a year old. We all know the signs: a child throws himself on the floor and wails, or he may turn around in circles, or beat his head against a wall, or stiffen like a board, or hold his breath.

In any event, it is an enormous expenditure of energy, which the child musters as an outward sign that he is frustrated and would like you to notice. (I have never known of a child who put forth this amount of energy without an audience.)

Of course, the best answer for a tantrum is to try to avoid it. The conscious parent tries to anticipate and looks for signs of fatigue and frustration. She makes a quick change of plans, diverts the attention, or stops to give a hug or reassurance if she sees that the child is getting ready to lose it.

However, tantrums are not always avoidable. When a child throws one, several principles need to be remembered:

He should not, under any circumstances, be rewarded for his effort by getting what he wanted. (Of course, this would only teach him to throw tantrums whenever he wanted something.)

If possible, the adults should move away from the child, staying within view, but far enough so that they can resume their activities and conversations—in quiet tones—as if they are deaf and blind to the tantrum.

If it is not safe to leave the child, or if this whole predicament is totally embarrassing to you (as in a grocery store, church, doctor's office, or mall), pick the child up—without a word—and carry him screaming to a safe place (another room, the car, outdoors). Carefully put him down and say, once, quietly, "When you are finished, we can talk." Then move away, but stay within view. (You might stand outside the car.)

When the child has calmed himself down, hug him, hold

him, comfort him. Validate his feelings. "I know that must have made you tired. I understand that you are unhappy. I'm sorry that life is hard sometimes, and it doesn't seem fair. Let me know when you are ready to try again."

Of course, if the tantrum starts up again, you would need to repeat the measures outlined above.

Grandparents

Grandparents can be God's gift to children. They are usually the only people in the world, beside the parents, who will actually place the good of the child ahead of their own good. They are sometimes the best source of unconditional love for their grandchild. Because they have more wisdom and more experience, their vision is usually a little clearer when it comes to knowing what is important for children and what isn't. They often have more patience and more time than the parents have, and they can be a tremendous support and cheerleader in the child's life.

Sometimes grandparents and parents do not agree on child rearing methods. This can be a source of tension.

If you are lucky, you can discuss your differences and decide who will be in charge of the decisions about children when you are together. It might be wise to let grandparents set the rules in their house, and parents set the rules at home.

However, if being together causes unbearable tension, it might be wise to let the grandparents baby-sit with your children when you are otherwise occupied. This is a good excuse to have a date with your spouse. (It is reassuring to children to know that their parents enjoy each other's company and still like to be alone.)

Sometimes grandparents show partiality to one child. This is very hard on parents and on the other children. It is wise for you to confront the issue so that it will not develop into a full-fledged boulder. Perhaps a third party could help you discuss the matter if dialogues in the past have proved to be unsuccessful.

Don't deny your children the wonderful experience of grandparents (unless they are abusive). It won't hurt your children to be indulged every now and again. They will learn soon enough that all adults are different and have different expectations. Their lives will be richer because they were privileged to enjoy the kind of love only grandparents can give.

The conscious parent takes seriously the responsibility to build a child's self-esteem, excitement for learning, and sense of autonomy. The most lasting contribution we will ever make in this world is that of affecting the life of a child. Therefore, as parents, we need to continually reassess our own lives and set worthy goals for our own behavior, knowing that the future generation is walking in our footsteps.

For that reason I will strive to be . . .

BRAVE enough to say no when it would be easier to say yes to my child, especially when I know that my refusal will make me unpopular and him angry

PATIENT enough to let my child learn from his own mistakes

LOVING enough to let him suffer the consequences of his actions

HONEST enough to tell the truth when my child comes to me with a question

SENSITIVE enough to be there when he needs me

INTELLIGENT enough to realize that he has much to teach me if I will only be willing to learn

DETERMINED enough to listen more and talk less, especially when my child is trying to tell me something

ACCEPTING enough to realize that my child is a separate person with needs, qualities, strengths, and weaknesses unlike me and unique to him

BIG enough to apologize when I jump to conclusions or blame someone else when the fault is mine

COURAGEOUS enough to take a good look in the mirror and honestly evaluate the self I see

SELF-DISCIPLINED enough to attempt to master new goals

STRONG enough to put forth the effort to become the person of my dreams

TOLERANT enough to accept weaknesses and shortcomings in others without griping or belittling them

SECURE enough to look for and affirm the good I see in others

CAPABLE enough to cope with daily obstacles, attempting to solve problems and not just complain about them

COMPASSIONATE enough to show respect to younger and older people by sacrificing time and energies for them

KIND enough to be concerned about the needs of others

WISE enough to remember that if I want my child to grow up to possess these noble traits, it will be necessary for him to see them first in me.

Appendix A

Ideas for Incentives to Be Used at Home

Activities for Young Children

Painting or drawing
Talking on the phone
Playing with toys
Playing in the puppet theater
First choice of a car seat
Using clay
Listening to the record player or tape recorder
Sitting in a special chair
Daydreaming; looking out the window
Going for a walk with a parent
Playing a favorite game
Watching a motion picture
Helping with dinner or special treat

Emptying garbage cans
Cleaning tables at lunchtime
Running errands
Sitting beside the teacher at lunch
Using special markers saved for fancy occasions
Checking the mailbox
Having a party
Making a collage
Making instant pudding, a popcorn necklace, finger puppets
Threading beads
Doing mosaic artwork using rice, peas, beans
Sharing a picture book with grandma on a cassette tape
Playing parent for a day
Taking a nature walk outside
Feeding the fish
Being the Indian chief—get to wear headdress
Having story read to the child
Getting first-place ribbons, special pins/buttons
Getting ice cream or cookie
Phone child's grandparent(s) and tell them what a great helper the
    child is
Inviting a lunch visitor
Having a popcorn party
Doing puzzles
Making thumbprints with an ink pad
Making pictures with construction paper scraps
Getting certificates, or coupons worth free chore
Inviting a teacher or friend to spend some time

Activities for Older Children

Playing a favorite game
Watching a motion picture
Doing artwork such as painting, drawing, working with clay
Selling raffle tickets for charity

Recording a story on the tape recorder and playing it for the family or a sibling
Working outside
Having extra time for enjoyable activities
Helping at someone else's house
Inviting a visitor to lunch
Getting "no chore" passes
Sending letters to grandparents
Getting certificates, badges
Having Coke breaks (certain day, certain time)
Playing sports
Listening to favorite songs on tape
Going to the library
Cleaning windows or dusting
Making a placemat that will be laminated
Doing only half of a chore
Having extra reading time or TV time
Reading stories to younger children
Doing science experiments in the kitchen
Sharing special talent or interest with family
Preparing seasonal artwork for the front door
Getting ribbons and pins to wear
Going on a field trip with the family
Being parent for a day
Having free time to listen to music and read a book
Writing poetry
Playing games, word search
Listening to the radio with headphones
Having special dress-up days (punk rock, mix match, etc.)
Later bedtime

Activities for Teens

Getting a chore coupon
Planning a family outing and organizing all details

Running video camera
Making puppets and putting on a show
Helping move equipment
Watering plants
Having extra time for break
Being exempt from housework
Listening to radio with headphones
Helping make popcorn for football games
Working on special family project or personal scrapbook
Earning special time to participate in club activities
Extra time to socialize
Going to a dance
Having a party
Tutoring students
Getting a later bedtime
Being able to bring food, drinks, a radio, etc. into bedroom
Getting a treat at the end of each satisfactory week
Looking at interesting magazines
Choosing restaurant for take-out food
Planning and/or preparing special meal

Appendix B

What to Say (or Do) When Parents Abuse Their Children in Public*

"He seems to be trying your patience."

"Is he tired? Does he need a nap?"

Find something positive to say about the child to the parent, i.e., "Your child is beautiful," or "What pretty hair she has."

"My child used to get upset like that."

"Children can wear you out, can't they? Is there anything I can do to help?"

Strike up a conversation with the adult. See if you can redirect his/her attention away from the child.

Sympathize with the parent, i.e., "Isn't it amazing how children think they can get what they want by kicking and screaming?"

*Produced by Dr. Katharine C. Kersey for the Child Abuse Prevention Month Coalition.

"My son behaves like that sometimes, and I . . ."

If you are concerned about the physical safety of the child, alert the store manager.

Divert the child's attention (if he is misbehaving), by talking to him, engaging him in conversation.

Praise child and/or parent at first opportunity.

If the child is in danger, offer assistance. For example, if the child was left unattended in a grocery cart, go stand by the child until the parent returns.

If you have authority over the parent, say, "This is a safe environment for children. We do not spank here."

Talk empathically to the child, i.e., "You're tired and really want to go home," or "You have spent a lot of time in that cart and now you want to get out."

Carry with you "Tips for Shopping with Children." Give one to the parent.

If you know the parent, offer to watch the child while she/he takes a break, gets a drink, etc.

What to Do in the Grocery Store to Help Children Behave . . . Without Spanking, Hitting or Yelling*

Give the child a responsibility. (Help select the hardest apples, find the cheapest green beans, match the coupons with the labels.)

Ignore inappropriate behavior unless it is dangerous, destructive, or embarrassing to you or a bother to others.

If a child gets out of control (temper tantrum) or embarrasses you, stop, pick him up (or take him by the hand), and take him out of the store, or to the rest room (to a private place), talk to him quietly, eye to eye, and tell him that his behavior is totally inappropriate. If necessary, put him in the backseat of the car and stay beside the car or sit in the front seat, saying nothing else. Wait for him to calm down, no matter how long it takes. Then ask him if he is ready to

*Produced by Dr. Katharine C. Kersey in cooperation with Parents Anonymous of Virginia, Inc. See your local grocer about making these tips available in ads, on bags, and/or at the register.

try again. (If he doesn't calm down, take him home. Find a sitter. Leave him there while you return to the store.)

Praise another child's appropriate behavior.

Play a game with the child. (Let's count all the tennis shoes we see on people's feet; let's see how many Bs you can find on signs.)

Let's guess how much something is going to cost.

Before entering the store, discuss rules: "No junk foods. When we leave, you can select a package of gum if you remember the rules."

Bring a nutritious snack (raisins, cut-up apples, nuts, etc.) for child to eat during the shopping trip.

Bring a story book for the child to look at.

With the child, develop a sign language at home. Use signals that mean, "Stop," "Come here," and "Be careful." Use them in public. Children are very responsive and strangers are impressed.

Don't let the child out of your sight. Hold hands. Let him hold onto or help steer the grocery cart.

Reinforce appropriate behavior. Talk with him, play with him, engage him in decision-making processes. Encourage him to talk, watch, listen, think.

Bring a favorite blanket, toy, or book from home to help make him feel secure.

Don't bring children who are tired or hungry to the store. Arrange for a baby-sitter.

Role play at home how to act in the grocery store. Go when you are rested, as well as when the child is rested. Don't wait until the end of a tiring day.

Sing songs with the child. Make up a grocery store song.

Give the child something of yours to play with such as keys, pocketbook, or note pad and pencil.

Tell the child you will have to leave him at home next time, then **do** it.

Stop unacceptable behavior as soon as it occurs. Don't ignore behavior that is dangerous, destructive, or embarrassing. Don't let the child think that you will allow him to misbehave in public.

Make a game out of it. Who can see the potatoes first? Do you remember what animal bacon comes from? If the child is old enough, let him check the grocery list and see which fruit, cheese, etc. is the best bargain.

Discuss the pictures on the packages. What could your child make with them?

Let your child know ahead of time that you will stop by the park on the way home or play a game with him when you get home if he behaves nicely at the store. Intersperse the shopping with fun activities, where you sit and have a talk, play a game, etc.

Don't ever buy the child a treat from the store where he threw a fit.

Keep a supply of little action figures or small manipulative toys handy.

For a small child, tie a favorite soft toy to the handle of the shopping cart.

Let the child see how many things one can do with a certain item (i.e., what you can make out of tomato paste).

Find five things on each aisle that start with letter B, are red, are in cans, are for eating, and not for eating, etc.

Count how many steps it takes to get from the Cheerios to the Frosted Flakes.

Do "quiet cheers" at the checkout stand, spelling each child's name: "Give me an A(A), give me an M(M)," etc.

While waiting in line, retell your child's favorite story having him chime in on the verses he knows.

With a toddler, play modified "catch" with an apple while he sits in the basket.

Play "I see something" in the checkout lane and have the children guess what you see.

Describe a food in the cart and have the children guess the food.

Have the child help you name all the vegetables in the cart, all the meats, breads, fruits, milk products.

Wear comfortable shoes and clothes to the grocery (both parent and child). Stay warm.

As your child is able, let her comparison shop for you. ("Which is the cheapest? Which gives you more for your money?")

Praise, praise, praise your child whenever he is doing something right!

Take an older child (neighbor's child) with you. He might like the diversion and be able to distract and entertain your child.

Ask the store manager to remove gum, candy, and toys from the checkout lines.

Go shopping with a friend. Children are usually better behaved when we are happier and when we are more relaxed and creative.

Make a behavior chart before you leave home. Engage the child in buying stickers and deciding on rewards. Remind him before you go into the store of his behavior chart.

Appendix D

Ideas for Family Behavior Charts

My Potty Chart

When your child is ready to be potty trained, make a chart with bears on it. Cut out little sets of underwear from old, worn-out underwear and put Velcro on the bears' bottoms and on the underwear. Every time the child has a success in the potty, he gets to put underwear on a bear. When all the underwear is on the bears, he gets to call Grandmother and tell her about his new accomplishment.

STEPHANIE
&
STACEY

Behavior to be reinforced: Not coming into mom's room at night.

Short term reward: A PIECE OF PIZZA TO PUT IN PAN

Long term reward: Going out to pizza place!

Stop Sleeping in Parent's Bed

When children have become accustomed to sleeping with their mom, and you decide that you want to stop this practice, you might make a pizza pie with cut-out pieces of pizza. Each night a child stays in her room all night, she gets to put a slice of pizza in the pizza pan (fastened with Velcro). When all the pizza is in the pan, the family makes pizza, orders it out, or goes to a pizza parlor.

CHRISTOPHER'S CHART
" I stayed in bed all night !!! "

"I Stayed in My Bed All Night"

If your child has trouble staying in his bed at night, draw a picture of a bed and block it off into sections. Buy some stickers that he can place on a section every morning if he has stayed in his bed the whole night. When all the bed is filled with stickers, he may be given a nickel for each one. He can go with you to the store to select a toy or prize.

Piano Practice Chart

For a child who is supposed to practice the piano, it might work to make a chart with a piano like the bed chart above and get some musical stickers (or draw musical notes). For each twenty minutes of practice, a section is filled. When the whole piano is filled with stickers, a long-awaited item is bought.

This kind of chart can be used for homework or reading books, too. For twenty minutes of homework or reading, a sticker is placed on the chart. When the whole chart is full, a desired item is bought for the child.

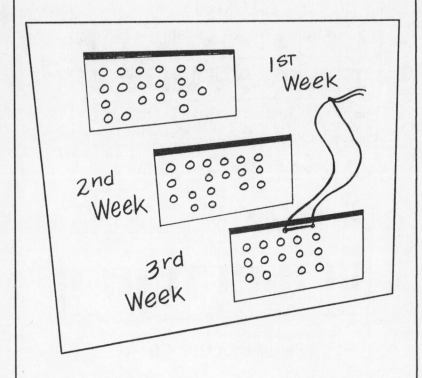

Hole Punches

Hole punches and $3'' \times 5''$ cards work beautifully when wanting to chart a new behavior. Lavishly give hole punches whenever the child behaves in a certain manner. An agreed-upon reward is bestowed after a designated number of hole punches.

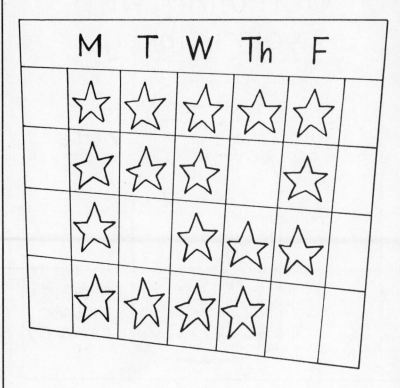

Mommy Yelling Chart

When Mom wants to stop yelling, she can reward herself with a point for every one-third of the day she goes without yelling. When she has three points, she gets to put a sticker on the calendar chart. When she has five stickers, the family cooks dinner for her.

Quibbling with Your Sibling

In order to help children focus on kind words and acts, encourage them to put a peanut in the jar every time they remember to say or do something kind or thoughtful for another family member. When the peanuts are up to a certain level, the family bakes cookies together. When they reach another level, everyone rents a movie. When the jar is full, the family spends the day at the park.

Arlene's Get Up & Get Ready Chart

	MON	TUES	WED	THUR	FRI	MON	TUES	WED	THUR	FRI	MON	TUES	WED	THUR	FRI
GET UP W/OUT CRYING		●	●	●			●	●	●	●	●	●	●	●	●
MAKE BED	●		●		●	●	●	●		●	●	●	●	●	
GET DRESSED	●	●	●	●	●		●	●	●	●	●	●	●	●	●
EAT BREAKFAST	●		●	●	●		●	●	●	●		●	●	●	●
BRUSH TEETH		●	●	●			●		●	●	●	●	●	●	●
COMB HAIR	●	●	●	●	●		●	●	●	●	●	●	●	●	●

Arlene's Get Up and Get Ready Chart

To have a seven-year-old get herself ready for school before 7:30 A.M., make a chart where she can draw a red dot for each job completed. When she has a certain number of dots, she will receive something she has been wanting. When a larger number of dots are on the chart, the entire family will go to Grandma's house.

Bears on a Chart

If the teacher says Sara is not getting her seat work done at school, make a set of "bear" cards for her to take to school. Ask the teacher to send one of them home with Sara every day she completes her assignment. At home, the cards can be placed on a calendar. When a number have been collected, Sara can have the new shoes she has been wanting.

Quality Time with Mom

Busy parents who want to be sure they spend fifteen minutes a day with each child can make charts to help make this a habit. For each day the goal is accomplished, a sticker is placed on the chart by the child. When the desired number has been earned, Dad and Mother spend a weekend together, and Grandmother keeps the kids.

Star Chart

Your child is given a card with a star drawn on it. The child is rewarded for appropriate behavior by being allowed to use special markers to color in one point of their star. When all five points are filled in, the child picks a prize out of a prize box or is given a special privilege (like staying up 30 minutes later, choosing the TV program, having one extra story read to him, or time to play a game with you).

You Were Caught Being Good

Get the whole neighborhood into the act! These tickets are issued by all members of the neighborhood to any child in the neighborhood "caught being good." These tickets are used by the children to purchase prizes or admittance to special neighborhood parties or activities.

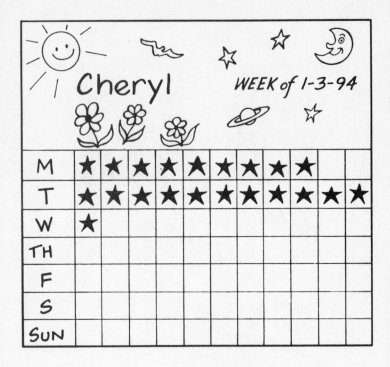

Weekly Chart

Make a weekly chart for your child. Stars can be earned on the chart in two ways: one point for completing a chore or request, and another for behaving appropriately and cooperatively while doing so. Several points could be earned each day. When your child has earned forty points by the end of the week, let him or her choose a prize from a box and send his or her chart to grandparents, who may also reward the behavior with a phone call or gift.

Worm Chart

Each time a member of the family is observed behaving appropriately, they receive a segment of the worm to place on the bulletin board or chart in the kitchen or family room. When the worm is completed (twenty pieces), the family is rewarded with a special activity, movie, or special treat.

Monthly Theme Chart

Tape a construction paper heart to a chart in the kitchen or family room. When you observe your child behaving appropriately (catch them being good!), stick a star or sticker on her heart. When she earns ten stars, reward her with a small gift or privilege. Use a different shape each month (snowman in January, shamrock in March, etc.)

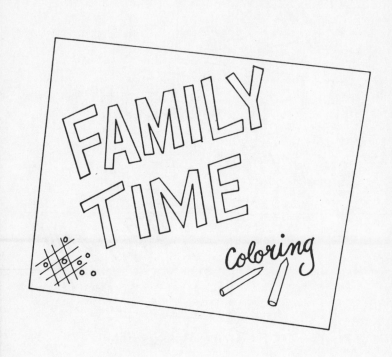

Family Time

Bright, decorative letters spelling "FAMILY TIME" are given as rewards. Each time your child or children behave appropriately or cooperatively at church, the doctor's office, grocery store, or mall, add another letter to the bulletin board in the kitchen or family room. When all ten letters are earned, the family receives a special activity or attends a family event.

Chore Passes

These tickets are given to children at the end of the day as a reward for their good behavior. The child signs his or her name to it and places it in the "Floating Chore" box (decorated shoe box with slit in the top). Every Friday or Sunday, you draw a ticket from the box and the child can be exempt from performing that chore for the week. For short-term improvement in performance of a household chore, the child could receive a "Chore Pass" each time he or she completes all the chores on time. After a specified length of time, your child may use the pass to be exempt from the chore for a week.

Super Sunbeam Tickets

Give tickets to your children for their good behavior throughout the day, particularly some specific behavior they are developing or improving. Whenever the children receive tickets, they sign the tickets and drop them in a big fish bowl placed somewhere in the kitchen or family room. On a specified day (every few days at first, then weekly) any number of tickets can be drawn from the bowl, and the children receive a prize, piece of candy, stickers, or some larger item they have been working for.

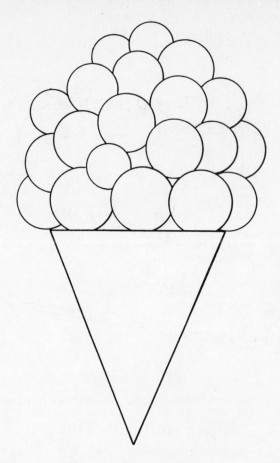

Ice Cream Chart

Tickets can simply be small colored circles that represent scoops of ice cream. Your child receives these tickets from you or any other member of the family. Your child is allowed the honor of adding it to his or her chart—a big cone with spaces for twenty scoops of ice cream. When the chart is filled, your child is rewarded with a trip to an ice cream parlor or an ice cream party with friends.

How to Build a Child's Self-esteem

Show children that you like them by smiling at them, hugging them, and speaking to them in a positive way.

Read out loud together as a family.

Use positive reinforcement to encourage responsible behavior.

Help them to learn responsibility by requiring them to complete tasks.

Set aside a time each day to spend with each child individually.

Help children to develop organizational skills by providing space for toys, books, etc.

Help them to discover their own special gifts by letting them develop an interest in activities such as sports, music, dance, etc.

Encourage their independence.

Get to know their teachers.

Do not embarrass children by yelling at them in public.

Try to help your child to achieve success in some way each day by offering a variety of activities.

Listen to your child and look him in the eyes when he is talking to you.

Do not set your expectations so high that the chance of failure prevents your child from trying.

Encourage your child to be proud of his name, his ideas, and his work. Pride makes a person try harder and strive to do better.

Give your child recognition for the effort he makes, even though it may not come up to your expectations. If you do this, the child will continue to try.

Answer your child's questions openly, honestly, and immediately, if possible.

Take your child with you on trips to run errands and involve him in some of the decision-making (i.e., "Should we go to the grocery store first or to Grandmother's first?").

Build a file of mementoes of things in which your child participated.

Point out and appreciate unique qualities in your child (skills, attitudes, behaviors, abilities, desires, etc.) that make him or her special to you and others.

Do not compare one child to another.

Allow your children to express their feelings and let them know it's OK to do so.

Use a democratic method of discipline. Children should be allowed to talk and parents should listen to what they have to say.

Let your child know that you love him even when you disapprove of his behavior.

When discipline is necessary, do so with love, using positive suggestions constructively rather than criticizing destructively.

Take time from work to eat lunch with your child or visit his school.

Let your child hear you praise him to other adults.

Welcome your children's friends into your home.

Appendix F

Positive Ways to Encourage Children's Growth

- Show children you like them. Welcome them with smiles, hugs, and comments when they wake up, come home from outings, school, etc. Listen to them when they talk, and show an interest in their ideas. Give them the respect and courtesy you wish to be shown.

- Provide a model for intellectual curiosity. Read to children when they are young, continue to read around them as they grow. Take them to the library and let them select books. Choose some for yourself, too. Get them involved in questioning, discussing, and problem-solving on a variety of subjects (domestic, mathematical, ethical, etc.)

- Reward responsible behavior and tasks you ask your children to complete. Positive reinforcement can be short-term rewards such as smiles, hugs, stickers, or small snacks, and long-term rewards can be trips to favorite places or social outings with friends. Provide opportunities for children to succeed by giving them age-appropriate tasks to help them achieve competence and mastery.

- Require your child to complete certain tasks starting at an early age. Try using the when/then technique and the concept, "If you abuse it, you lose it." Obviously, the privilege will be removed if the child fails to comply. Don't do his chores for him. Let him know the responsibility is his. Don't nag, scold, or complain.

- Set aside time each day (or at least each week) to give your child your undivided attention. Go for a walk or play a game with him. Create a climate where he can talk about anything on his mind. Listen.

- Encourage organization at an early age. Children who are provided with helpful arranged space, with a place for toys, art supplies, books, etc., will be ready and able to be organized about school belongings in the years to come.

- Help your child discover her natural gifts. Let her develop a special interest activity (drama, dance, sports); something about which she is very enthusiastic. Show your support of these extracurricular hobbies. They enlarge your child's circle of friends and help her feel more productive and special.

- Work with the teacher. Don't talk her down to the child. If you have questions, deal with her directly. Let the child know that you are supportive of the teacher's efforts.

- Encourage your child's growing independence and autonomy. As he grows older, help him realize that someday he will be his own boss and you have faith in his ability to figure things out and make rules for himself.